WERNHER VON BRAUN

WERNHER
VON BRAUN

CHRISTOPHER LAMPTON

AN IMPACT BIOGRAPHY

FRANKLIN WATTS
New York · London · Toronto · Sydney · 1988

Library of Congress Cataloging-in-Publication Data

Lampton, Christopher.
    Wernher von Braun.

    (An Impact biography)
    Bibliography: p.
    Includes index.
    Summary: Traces the life and achievements of German
rocket scientist Wernher Von Braun from his childhood
dreams of human interplanetary travel to their
realization as von Braun became a prominent figure in
modern rocketry.
    1. Von Braun, Wernher, 1912–1977—Juvenile literature.
2. Rocketry—Biography—Juvenile literature. [1. Von
Braun, Wernher, 1912–1977. 2. Engineers] I. Title.
TL781.85.V6L36 1988   629.4′092′4 [B] [92]   88-221
ISBN 0-531-10606-3

Photographs courtesy of: The Archives, Alabama
Space and Rocket Center, Huntsville, Alabama:
pp. 2, 14, 16, 19, 21, 27, 28, 33, 43, 99, 105, 112;
NASA: pp. 10, 116, 119, 126, 130, 138; UPI/
Bettmann Newsphotos: pp. 37, 38, 60, 75, 89, 122,
128; U.S. Air Force: p. 64.

Frontis: Dr. von Braun in his office as director of the
Marshall Space Flight Center in Huntsville, Alabama

CONTENTS

WERNHER VON BRAUN

PROLOGUE

On the morning of July 16, 1969, Wernher von Braun awoke before sunrise. His sleep had been restless. At 4 A.M. the fifty-seven-year-old rocket scientist rose, showered, dressed, and drove the short distance to Merritt Island, a spit of land on the Atlantic coast of Florida.

Ten years earlier, Merritt Island had been a mosquito-infested swamp. Now it was the site of the largest building in the world, the Vehicle Assembly Building (VAB), a structure so huge that it was air-conditioned to prevent indoor rain clouds from forming in its upper recesses.

Next to the Vehicle Assembly Building sat the smaller Launch Control Center, which von Braun entered in the predawn gloom. In the distance, obscured by darkness but given a ghostly visibility by the artificial lights that had burned throughout the night, von Braun could see the largest rocket ever built, the *Saturn 5*, towering above the island like a thirty-story building. Later that day, the *Saturn 5* would propel a crew of three men to the moon.

Inside a large room in the Launch Control Center, von Braun sat at a small console surrounded by more than fifty other workers. From time to time he looked up at a bank of television monitors, where he could view the massive rocket outside. The *Saturn 5* was the largest in a series of increasingly powerful rockets that von Braun had been building for nearly forty years,

since he had been a young man in college. It was far and away the most powerful. It would also be the last.

Von Braun might not have realized it at the time, but the *Saturn 5* marked the end of an era, even as it tentatively marked the beginning of a new era, that of human beings in space.

Perhaps, as he stared at the *Saturn 5* rocket on the television monitors, von Braun's mind went back into the past, traveling briefly over the long chain of events that had brought him to where he now stood. Did he think of the *V-2*, the first great war rocket that he had helped build during the frantic last days of World War II? Did he think of the *Juno* rocket that had launched the first American satellite, *Explorer 1*, into orbit around the earth? Did he think of the *Redstone*, which had lofted the first American into the fringes of outer space?

Or did he think of something darker, of the hellish Nazis for whom he had worked in a long-ago time and place? Did he think of Adolf Hitler, the malevolent ruler who had used von Braun's rockets to exact a terrible vengeance on the nations that had thwarted his plans for world conquest? Did he think of the innocent civilians who had died in England and other countries as his rockets rained down on their homes?

Or perhaps his mind went even farther back in time, to his earliest memories, to his home in a country then known as the German Empire . . .

The huge *Saturn 5* rocket, boosting the *Apollo 11* spacecraft into space and toward the moon, is launched on July 16, 1969.

1

"Here was a task worth dedicating one's life to."

The reign of the German Empire had been short, and it had ended with a bang.

In 1861, an empire led by the great statesman Otto von Bismarck had been forged out of a disparate collection of European principalities. It lasted forty-seven years, until Germany was defeated to end the First World War.

Germany's victorious enemies feared, and not without reason, that their fallen adversary might rise again phoenix-like from the ashes of war and reignite the conflict that had so recently ended. In hopes of rendering Germany permanently powerless, small pieces of it were given to other countries. What remained of the nation—still quite large, even so—was forced to abide by the rigorous terms of the Treaty of Versailles.

This left postwar Germany, now under a newly installed government called the Weimar Republic, in a state of chaos. Inflation ran wild, unemployment was rampant, and revolutionaries plotted in the streets. It was an unstable situation. Ultimately, it led to the very thing Germany's enemies had been trying to prevent—another war.

Wernher von Braun was born on March 23, 1912, two years before the First World War began. When it ended, he was barely six. To what extent the chaotic

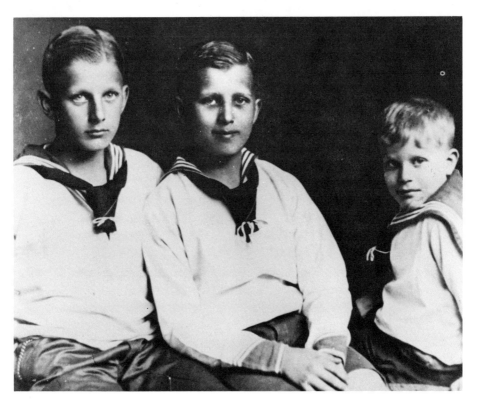

From left to right, the three von Braun brothers: Sigismund, Wernher, and Magnus

state of German politics affected young Wernher's childhood is difficult to say; probably not much. But as he grew to adulthood, the legacy of World War I and the Treaty of Versailles would return to shape his life in unexpected but profound ways.

Wernher was born to the aristocracy. His father was Baron Magnus von Braun, a wealthy farmer and minister of agriculture under the Weimar Republic. By all accounts, Wernher was a charming and attractive boy, given to intense but enduring enthusiasms. He had two brothers. Sigismund was a year older than Wernher; Magnus was seven years his junior.

Like certain other individuals who later went on to

have brilliant careers in science—Albert Einstein is an example—Wernher was a mediocre student in the sciences. Perhaps his poor grades resulted from a lack of motivation. Young Wernher saw no reason to learn math or physics. They had no relevance to his life. Until he discovered rocketry . . .

Rocketry was a fad in Germany during the 1920s. In theory, a rocket is nothing more than a chamber filled with hot gas, with a small hole at one end. As the hot gas expands and rushes out of the hole, the chamber flies in the opposite direction, according to Isaac Newton's Third Law of Motion (for every action there is an equal and opposite reaction). The ancient Chinese used rockets in fireworks, as they are still used today; in the eighteenth and nineteenth centuries, the British used them as weapons of war. (American poet Francis Scott Key immortalized the British war rocket when he wrote about "the rocket's red glare, the bombs bursting in air" in the war of 1812—lines that eventually became part of the American national anthem.)

War rockets fell out of favor around 1850, replaced by more powerful conventional artillery. But interest in rocketry was revived in the early twentieth century, when a Russian schoolteacher named Konstantin Tsiolkovsky suggested that rockets could boldly go where no other form of human transportation could—into outer space. Because the rocket is a purely reactive device, acting according to Newton's law, it can travel through an airless vacuum, with nothing to "push against." Tsiolkovsky envisioned a future in which people flew to the moon in rocketships and lived in cylindrical space colonies orbiting the earth.

In the 1920s, a Transylvanian mathematician named Hermann Oberth published a book entitled *Die Rakete zu den Planetenraumen* (*The Rocket into Interplanetary Space*), in which he explained the mathematical and physical theory behind rocket flight in some detail. It

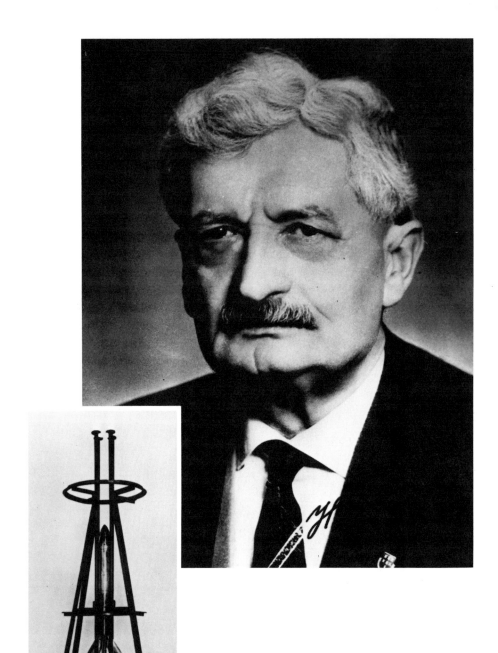

Dr. Hermann Oberth, German rocket pioneer. *Inset:* An early Oberth rocket on its test stand, ready for firing.

was a difficult book for the nonscientifically minded to understand, but it did include a lucid description of spaceflight via rocket. In 1925, it found its way into the hands of thirteen-year-old Wernher von Braun.

The enthusiastic young Wernher already knew a thing or two about rockets. He had followed with some interest the exploits of a rocket experimenter named Max Valier, who had teamed with automobile-maker Fritz Von Opel to build hybrid rocket cars—automobiles propelled by rockets—in which Valier set speed records on a track near Berlin. Inspired by Valier's example, the young von Braun built his own rocket car by attaching several fireworks rockets to a coaster wagon and setting them off all at once. The experiment was a success . . . up to a point.

"I was ecstatic," von Braun recalled much later. "The wagon was wholly out of control and trailing a comet's tail of fire, but my rockets were performing beyond my wildest dreams." Alas, the out-of-control wagon veered into Berlin's most crowded thoroughfare, the *Tiergarten Strasse*, and young Wernher was arrested. "Fortunately, no one had been injured, so I was released in charge of the Minister of Agriculture—who was my father."[1]

Wernher was also aware of space travel, in theory, at least. In his leisure time, he devoured the science fiction novels of writers such as Jules Verne and H. G. Wells and dreamed of the faraway worlds that they wrote about. Later, on his fourteenth birthday, his mother, an amateur astronomer, gave him a telescope, with which he could directly study the stars and planets.

But it was Oberth's book that brought the two concepts of rocketry and space travel together in von Braun's mind. For the first time, he realized that space travel might be more than an exciting fantasy, that it might actually be *possible* for humans to travel among the planets and stars. And, inevitably, he saw himself as the person who would build the rockets that would send explorers into outer space. Perhaps he would one day travel to the moon himself. Without fully realizing it, the thirteen-year-old dreamer had just mapped out his life's career; forty-four years later he would indeed send explorers to the moon. He would never—alas—be able to make the trip himself, though he would never stop dreaming of the possibility.

Von Braun described his youthful infatuation to a reporter many years later: "It filled me with a romantic urge. Interplanetary travel! Here was a task worth devoting one's life to! Not just to stare through a telescope at the moon and the planets but to soar through the heavens and actually explore the mysterious universe! I knew how Columbus had felt."[2]

There had always been a bit of Columbus in von Braun, but there was also more than a bit of the engineer. Restless for some form of transportation better than his bicycle, he had once tried to build his own (nonrocket-propelled) car, before his father, infuriated by his poor grades, had put an end to the project and shipped him off to boarding school.

But building a moon rocket was engineering of a higher order. After a consultation with one of his teachers, von Braun realized that his ambitions would require that he grapple more seriously with the dreaded subjects of math and physics.

Grapple he did. Within a year he had risen to the top of his class at the Hermann Lietz School on Spiekeroog Island, in Germany's North Sea. Anxious to further his study of astronomy, he persuaded the principal of the school to purchase a moderately large telescope—a preview, it has been suggested, of von Braun's later ability to persuade governments to invest large sums of money in rocketry and space travel.

So successful was von Braun in his academic endeavors that he was given the opportunity to graduate

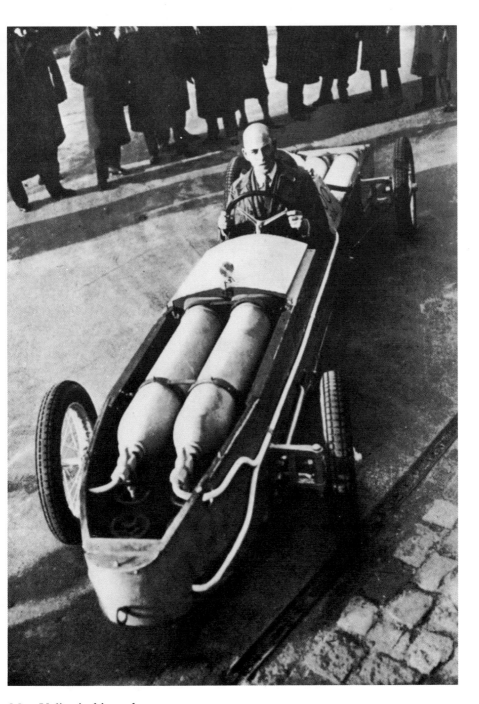

Max Valier in his rocket car

from high school a year early, and in his final year, when his mathematics teacher was taken ill, von Braun, himself a student in the class, was called upon to replace him. Apparently, he did the job well. Not one of the students, including von Braun himself, flunked the official math examination at year's end.

After graduation, von Braun attended the Charlottenburg Institute of Technology, in Berlin. As part of his education there, he apprenticed at a machine factory called the Borsig Works. And there he received his first practical education in what being an engineer really meant.

The foreman at the Works, a gruff, old-fashioned sort with glasses and a mustache, handed von Braun a chunk of iron, described as being "as large as a child's head,"[3] and instructed him to turn the chunk of iron into a perfect cube, with every face smooth, equal, and at right angles to every other face.

Make the iron into a cube? This was useless work as far as Wernher was concerned; there were more important jobs to be done, machines to be built, experience to be gained. Annoyed, von Braun stalked away and began filing at the iron. After a few days he had produced what he believed was a reasonably well-made cube. The foreman disagreed, however, or at least his standards were higher than his apprentice's. He ordered the young man to keep filing. More annoyed than ever, von Braun did so, this time spending three weeks at the job. But, once again, the foreman rejected the resulting cube as being imperfect.

Von Braun returned to filing. "Five weeks passed," he later recalled. "Each day my block grew smaller. My fingers were raw. But I was determined to produce a cube he would not reject. Finally I handed him my supreme effort. It was slightly larger than a walnut. Peering over his dusty glasses, he measured every side.

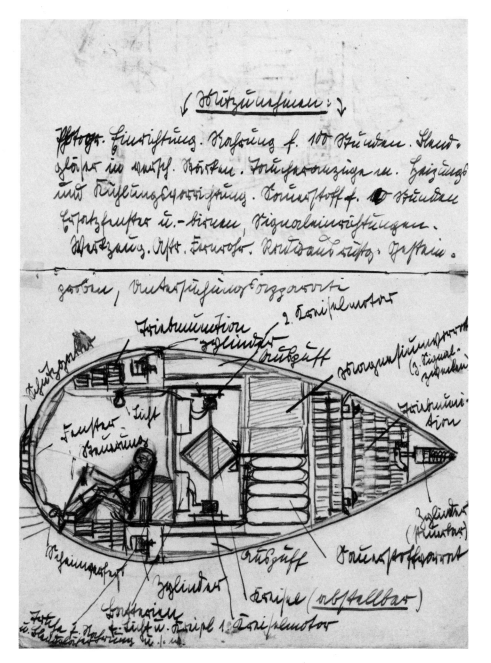

This sketch of a spacecraft was taken from a school workbook of von Braun's. He was fifteen or sixteen at the time.

My heart pounded. My reward was expressed in one word: "*Gut!* [*Good!*]"[4]

The young man had learned his lesson. A good engineer worked to exacting standards, even when meeting those standards required long hours of tedious work. The lesson would stand him in good stead years later, when the lives of astronauts would depend on the performance of his rockets, each of which was built from millions of precision parts.

The years at the Charlottenburg Institute were decisive ones in von Braun's life, not just because of the education he received but because in Berlin the young engineer discovered an organization that would have a profound influence on his future: the *Verein fur Raumschiffahrt* (Society for Space Travel), VfR for short.

The VfR had been founded in 1927. Early members included Hermann Oberth, the author of *The Rocket into Interplanetary Space*; Willy Ley, who would later move to the United States and become a major historian of rocketry; and Max Valier, the rocket car experimenter. Even before von Braun discovered the organization in 1930, it had had a fascinating and rather checkered history.

In 1929 Oberth, the president of the VfR, had been approached by a film company called UFA with a decidedly odd proposition. UFA was producing a science fiction movie entitled *Frau im Mond* (*The Woman in the Moon*), which would feature a rocket trip to the moon. Oberth was well known for his knowledge of rocket theory. Would he like to build a rocket that could be launched in time for the movie's premiere, to publicize the film?

Oberth jumped at the chance. The film company would finance the project, or so it said. Ultimately, most of the money would come from Oberth's own pocket, and from the pocket of the film's director, Fritz Lang.

Not that Oberth would keep his own end of the bargain. The rocket itself would never be completed.

The truth was that although Oberth was a great mathematician, he was a lousy engineer. (As an acquaintance once put it: "If Oberth wants to drill a hole, first he invents the drill press."[5]) Recognizing his own deficiencies, Oberth set about hiring a pair of assistants, neither of whom, as it turned out, was any more competent at engineering than he was. One of them, who would later figure prominently in the membership of the VfR, began his job interview with the words "Name is Rudolf Nebel, engineer with diploma, member of oldest Bavarian student corps, World War combat pilot with rank of lieutenant and eleven enemy planes to my credit."[6] Nebel's engineering talent turned out to be less than spectacular, but he had other talents, as von Braun and the rest of the VfR would later learn.

When the rocket, which Oberth had dubbed the *Kegeldeuse* ("cone-shaped"), failed to materialize, Oberth vanished from Berlin, later claiming to have suffered a nervous breakdown. The film premiere went on without him—and without the rocket launching. It was during this period that von Braun joined the VfR.

Actually, the VfR was something of a disappointment for von Braun. When he had first heard about the organization, he had visualized a grand society of scientists who sat in a great auditorium and discussed weighty matters of rocketry and space travel. But when he attended his first meeting he found a group of six men sitting in a lawyer's office, trying to figure out where they would get the money to build rockets. It was another lesson for the young engineer in the difference between the ideal and the practical, between the world as he had imagined it and the world as it really was.

Just as he had accepted the lesson of the iron cube at the Borsig Works, von Braun accepted the lesson of the VfR and soon became one of its most enthusiastic members. Rudolf Nebel, too, had risen to the top ranks of the organization, such as they were, in the short time he had been a member. What Nebel lacked as an engineer, he more than compensated for as a salesman; he had an extraordinary knack for raising money and wangling deals, keeping the VfR afloat on a minimum of resources. Some of his style must have rubbed off on the young von Braun, who would show a similar aptitude for salesmanship in later life.

By publicizing itself relentlessly, the VfR grew to an astounding 900 members by the end of 1930, though the number who actually attended meetings was much smaller. But the organization still lacked direction. The membership decided that it was time to build a rocket.

With what little money they had, the VfR purchased the unfinished rocket Oberth had constructed for the *Frau im Mond* premiere, which had subsequently become the property of the film company. Oberth was invited back to put the rocket engine into working order. As a publicity stunt, the rocket would be tested in the window of a downtown Berlin department store, after Nebel convinced the management of the store that the gimmick would be good for sales. (The rocket demonstration, as it turned out, increased the store's sales little, if at all, but neither did it attract funding to the VfR, as Nebel had hoped it would.)

Oberth agreed to participate in the stunt. Von Braun was ecstatic. Oberth had been his personal hero since he had read *The Rocket into Interplanetary Space* at thirteen, and now he was determined to become Oberth's assistant in the experiments. Willy Ley introduced von Braun to Oberth and apparently the mathematician was impressed, not only by von Braun's knowledge of rocketry and engineering, which by this time was considerable, but by his sheer enthusiasm for the subject.

Von Braun got the job. Standing in the middle of

downtown Berlin, building a rocket with a scientist that he idolized, explaining the experiment to crowds of curious bystanders, all this provided very much the right milieu for the young engineer. It exercised what were already emerging as von Braun's two greatest talents: building rockets and spreading his enthusiasm for rocketry to others.

The rocket itself—the *Kegeldeuse*—was rather unimpressive. No larger than a soda bottle, it consisted of two parts: a chamber to hold the hot gas that propelled the rocket; and a nozzle at the end, where the exhaust rushed out of the chamber. This contraption was attached to a flask of liquid oxygen and a tank of gasoline. The oxygen and gasoline were piped separately into the *Kegeldeuse* via copper tubes, where they were mixed together in the chamber and set on fire, producing the hot gas that rushed out of the nozzle. By keeping the oxygen and gasoline separate, the experimenters minimized the possibility of an accidental explosion—the gasoline needed the oxygen in order to burn—and maximized their ability to control the rocket's exhaust. Such liquid fuel rockets (as opposed to the solid fuel, gunpowder rockets of the Chinese and British) had first been proposed by Tsiolkovsky at the turn of the century and the idea had been elaborated on by Oberth in his book. The *Kegeldeuse* was intended to demonstrate that such rockets would work as predicted. (Unknown to the experimenters, working liquid fuel rockets had already been built on the other side of the Atlantic, by the American experimenter Robert Goddard.)

The *Kegeldeuse* never actually flew. It was designed to be fired downward into a bucket of water, which kept the rocket cool. Without the water, the rocket would have burned up from the heat of its own exhaust. The nozzle, pointing upward out of the water, presented a spectacular and noisy display of hot flames, but the rocket itself was held immobile by the bucket.

This arrangement, peculiar as it may seem, had a certain scientific justification. The power of a rocket—that is, its ability to lift things into the air—is called *thrust*. Thrust is measured in units of weight: pounds, grams, and so on. Roughly speaking, a rocket with one pound of thrust is capable of lifting one pound into the air, including its own weight and the weight of its fuel. By placing the bucket of water atop a grocer's scale and firing the *Kegeldeuse* downward into the bucket, the experimenters were able to measure the rocket's thrust—literally by *weighing* it—and thus they knew how much weight it would be able to carry if it actually flew.

The thrust of the *Kegeldeuse* was approximately 15 pounds (33 kg). Technically, the bucket and scale arrangement used by von Braun and Oberth was what rocket experimenters call a *test stand*. The stationary firing of a rocket in a test stand to measure its thrust (and other factors affecting the rocket's flight) is called *static firing*. As von Braun would discover during later experimentation with larger rockets, building a test stand was often as tricky as building the rockets themselves. Not only must the test stand be designed so as to measure the thrust of the rocket, but it must be strong enough to prevent the rocket from flying off into the air.

When the publicity stunt failed to generate extra funds, the VfR decided that the *Kegeldeuse* could be put to better use. They persuaded an organization called the *Chemisch-Technische Reichsanstalt* (Reich Institute for Chemistry and Technology) to test the rocket and issue an official certificate of performance, to prove that it performed as advertised. This they did, on a rainy July afternoon, with newspaper photographers present to record the event for posterity. But the certificate also failed to generate funds.

The first rocket built by von Braun. *Inset:* the rocket on its homemade test stand in Berlin in 1930.

Worse, an event occurred on May 17, 1930, that nearly stopped all German rocket experimenters in their tracks. Max Valier was killed when a rocket engine that he was building exploded, sending a splinter of steel into his heart. Since Valier was famous, the tragedy made front-page headlines, and rocket experimentation was nearly banned by the German government. Public pressure drove the VfR to move their experiments from Berlin to a small farm in the village of Bernstadt, where they worked on a new rocket that Nebel had designed called the *Mirak*, short for *Minimum-rakete* ("minimum rocket"). When this rocket, too, exploded—harming no one, fortunately—the group was driven back to Berlin, with no place left to experiment.

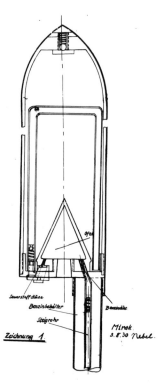

a diagram of the *Mirak*, designed by Rudolf Nebel

The ever-resourceful Nebel located an abandoned munitions dump in a suburb of Berlin called Reinickendorf and arranged with the city to rent the grounds for the trifling sum of ten *reichsmarks* (roughly $4) per year. The VfR dubbed the munitions dump the *Raketenflugplatz* (literally, "rocket-flying place"). The Great Depression of the 1930s was already in progress, and the streets of Berlin were full of unemployed workmen; Nebel lured large numbers of them—electricians, experts in handling sheet metal, and mechanics—to the *Raketenflugplatz* with promises of free meals, which he arranged to be picked up at a nearby soup kitchen that offered food to the unemployed. The workmen, who were utilized in rocket projects by the VfR, lived in abandoned buildings at the dump, as did Nebel. A cot was also put aside for von Braun, should he need to sleep over after a long day of experiments.

In the summer of 1931, von Braun moved briefly to Switzerland to study at the Federal Institute of Technology in Zurich. When he returned in the fall, Nebel had completed his first *Mirak*. It had been put together, at least in part, from materials Nebel had scrounged from local manufacturers. The clever Nebel had even arranged to charge admission to *Mirak* launches. The first firing, however, ended in total failure. The rocket did not even leave the launch pad. Later tests were more successful, and the VfR was soon encouraged to build a second, more advanced *Mirak*, called—naturally enough—*Mirak II*.

The VfR built another rocket as well, called the *Repulsor*, after a rocket in a science fiction novel that von Braun and Ley had read as teenagers. On one of the test firings of the *Repulsor* the rocket went wild and shot out of the *Raketenflugplatz*. Fearing that it would harm picnickers in the nearby forest—or perhaps worse, that it would crash into the local police barracks—the

VfR experimenters ran in wild pursuit of the rocket. Somewhat anticlimactically, they found that the rocket had lodged itself harmlessly in the limbs of a tall tree.

It was during one of the VfR's public rocket tests (Nebel was now regularly selling tickets to the launchings to raise funds) that fate intervened in the life of von Braun and others at the *Raketenflugplatz*. It took the form of an old ghost left over from World War I: the Treaty of Versailles.

2 "We were interested solely in exploring outer space."

As far as the German Army was concerned, World War I had never ended; it had just been put on hold. At the end of the war, the army had not been forced to sign a treaty of surrender, only to cease firing. The high command then sat back and waited for the day when the fighting would resume.

But Germany's enemies in the war had anticipated just such an attitude. Thus, the Treaty of Versailles put severe restrictions on the army's power: its size was limited, as were the number and variety of weapons that it could stockpile. In this way, Germany's enemies had hoped to prevent the nation from reviving the hostilities that ended in 1918. However, there were loopholes in the Treaty of Versailles, and one concerned rockets.

Rockets, in fact, were not mentioned in the treaty. By default, this meant that the army could build and stockpile as many rockets as it wanted. But rockets had not been used as weapons of war for nearly a century. Conventional artillery was vastly superior to the British war rockets of the 1800s, which could be fired over 2 or 3 miles (3.2 or 4.8 km) at best. By contrast, the so-called Paris Gun, a giant cannon used by the Germans during World War I, had a range of nearly 80 miles (120 km). As tactical weapons—which could be used

on the battlefield, against troops—rockets were hopelessly outclassed by rifles and cannon. As strategic
weapons—which could be used over long distances, like
the Paris Gun or the airplane—rockets showed some
promise, but no one had ever developed a true strategic
rocket.

Quietly, the German Army set out to do precisely
that, but it realized quickly that it would need help.
Why not take advantage, someone suggested, of the
vast pool of amateur rocket hobbyists who were forming
rocketry clubs across the nation?

The job of seeking out rocket inventors and bringing
the best of them under the wing of the army fell to the
Ballistics and Munitions Branch of the Army Weapons
Department. There was no shortage of such inventors
and experimenters in the Germany of the early 1930s,
but most of them were cranks of one sort or another.
Colonel Walter Becker, head of the Ballistics and Munitions Branch, and his assistant, thirty-five-year-old
Captain Walter Dornberger, were charged with sepa-
rating the wheat from the chaff, the bright young inventors from the cranks.

Eventually, this pair heard of the VfR. And, once
they had heard of it, it was inevitable that they would
find Wernher von Braun.

On a spring morning in 1932, Becker and Dornberger
drove to the *Raketenflugplatz* to watch a demonstration
of the *Mirak I*. They were not alone. A small crowd of
paying spectators watched along with them. But when
the ever-resourceful Nebel learned the identity of these
unusually well-dressed visitors, he persuaded them to
sign a contract giving the VfR 1,000 *Reichsmarks*
(roughly $400) to build the *Mirak II*, on the proviso
that they demonstrate it at the army's own proving
grounds, the Experimental Station West, located at
nearby Kummersdorf. The demonstration was sched-
uled for the following July.

General Walter Dornberger with Hermann Oberth in 1940. Dornberger would play a key role in Wernher von Braun's career.

When the appointed day came, von Braun and the other VfR members strapped the *Mirak* and its launching rack to the top of a car, loaded a second car with the rocket fuel and assorted paraphernalia, and drove to the proving grounds. As von Braun later described it:

[We] encountered Captain Dornberger at the rendezvous in the forests south of Berlin. Dornberger guided us to an isolated spot on the artillery range where were set up a formidable array of phototheodolites, ballistic cameras, and chronographs—instruments of whose very existence we had theretofore been unaware. The rocket was erected and fueled by two o'clock in the afternoon.

33

At the signal, *Mirak II* soared upward for a distance of some 200 feet. Here, however, its trajectory became almost horizontal so that the rocket crashed before the parachute could open.[7]

The army munitions men were disappointed; to them the *Mirak* seemed little more than a toy, and not an especially reliable one. Nebel asked for money for a second *Mirak* demonstration; he was refused. But by now the army munitions men had seen something that had impressed them far more than the *Mirak*: Wernher von Braun.

"I had been struck," Dornberger wrote later, "by the energy and shrewdness with which this tall, fair, young student with the broad massive chin went to work, and by his astonishing theoretical knowledge. It had seemed to me that he grasped the problems and that his chief concern was to lay bare the difficulties. In this respect he had been a refreshing change from most of the leading men at the place [that is, in the VfR]. When General [formerly Colonel] Becker later decided to approve our Army establishment for liquid-propellant rockets, I had put Wernher von Braun first on my list of proposed technical assistants."[8]

Unaware of this, the VfR sent von Braun back to Kummersdorf to ask Colonel Becker for additional money. Becker refused the request. It was his feeling that the VfR was more interested in selling tickets to *Mirak* launchings than in building better rockets. But he made von Braun and the other VfR members an offer: He would finance the rocket experiments of any one of them who wanted to perform those experiments under the aegis of the army, at the Kummersdorf test site, rather than at the *Raketenflugplatz*. In addition, Becker suggested that von Braun go back to school and earn an advanced degree. If von Braun wanted to write his doctoral thesis on a subject pertaining to rockets, the Kummersdorf facilities, which included the vast array of rocket-testing devices the VfR had seen on its first visit, would be available to him. Astounded by his good fortune, von Braun accepted the offer.

Nebel, however, had other ideas. As desperate as the VfR was for funds, he wasn't willing to sell out to the army. Other members of the VfR agreed with him, though several of them would end up in the employ of the army before the decade was over.

Nebel and the others did not know that the future of the VfR was limited. Two years later it would be disbanded under pressure, blown away by the shifting winds of German politics. Even as von Braun cast his lot with the army to build bigger and better rockets, a new party was rising in German politics, the National Socialist Party. It would soon be known to the world by a shorter version of that name: the Nazis.

In 1932, German politics were in turmoil, much as they had been after World War I, but now the turmoil was exacerbated by the worldwide depression that had followed in the wake of the American stock market crash of 1929. The year 1932 saw a forty-three-year-old revolutionary named Adolf Hitler almost elected president of Germany on the Nazi Party ticket. The following year, Hitler was appointed chancellor of the German nation, and shortly afterward he seized full dictatorial powers, declaring himself *Fuhrer* ("leader").

Hitler came to power by promising a return to the powerful Germany that had existed before World War I and the crippling Treaty of Versailles. But he also appealed to an odd streak of hatred that ran through a portion of the German populace. He preached intolerance toward minorities, especially Jews. He was a small-minded man with a peculiar charisma and the ability to drive crowds into a shouting frenzy with ranting, impassioned speeches. Many of the Nazi officials that he kept by his side were little better than thugs.

Some, like Hitler himself, had prison records, but to more than a few people they looked like the saviors of a weakened German nation.

Hitler formed about himself an elite guard, a personal army, separate from the German Army for which von Braun worked. It was called the SS—short for *Schutzstaffel*, or "protective squad." The SS were not only soldiers; they were armed bullies who ran the hideous concentration camps in which Hitler would ultimately incarcerate and murder millions of those whom he considered enemies of his imagined German "superrace," including millions of Jews whose only crime was their religion. The SS was controlled by the deceptively mild-mannered Heinrich Himmler, who would one day figure significantly in von Braun's life.

In 1934, a group of Nazi pilots decided that they wanted to use the *Raketenflugplatz* as a training ground. The VfR refused to let them. Mysteriously, a water bill appeared from the city for 1,000 marks, an amount that the rocket experimenters could not afford to pay. They were told that a faucet in the basement of one of the buildings had been leaking for years; the expense was not covered by the VfR's contract with the city, though the city had never mentioned this before. Thus, the VfR lost its launching site, and the Nazi pilots gained a practice field.

By this time, however, von Braun was long departed from the VfR. He was building rockets for the army, which had not yet been subsumed into the apparatus of the Nazi Party. His father had lost his job as minister of agriculture when Hitler had come to power and had moved the family back to the country. Von Braun, however, had remained in Berlin, so that he could be near the test site in Kummersdorf. Being more interested in rockets than in politics, the young engineer paid little attention to the Nazi phenomenon as it swept across Germany. As he told an interviewer many years later,

The *Fuhrer* gives a speech to autoworkers in Germany in 1938.

Hitler with Heinrich Himmler (spectacles), head of the Gestapo, in 1939

"I think one should not blame a twenty-one-year-old boy for not having understood the significance of such political leaders much older than himself."[9]

If von Braun had little interest in politics—and therefore, presumably, little interest in fighting wars—why did he go to work for the army? Apparently, because it offered him a chance to realize his lifelong dream, which was to build rockets. But there is a contradiction here that might not be immediately obvious. Von Braun wanted to build rockets that would fly to the moon. The army, on the other hand, wanted to build rockets that would drop bombs on distant enemies. Von Braun's rockets were to be vehicles for exploration; the army's rockets were weapons of destruction.

How did the young von Braun reconcile this contradiction? As he told a reporter in 1950, after he had come to the United States, "We [young rocket builders] needed money, and the army seemed willing to help us. In 1932, the idea of war seemed to us an absurdity. The Nazis weren't yet in power. We felt no moral scruples about the possible future abuse of our brain child. We were interested solely in exploring outer space. It was simply a question with us of how the golden cow would be milked most successfully."[10]

From our distant vantage point in the late twentieth century, this seems at once remarkably naive and remarkably cynical, but the young von Braun does not seem to have been a cynic. Probably, he assumed that any problems would take care of themselves in time; perhaps he genuinely believed that the army would in time finance a space rocket. In fact, this might not have been as naive a vision as it appears today: years later, von Braun launched the first American space satellite while working for the U.S. Army.

But things would not work out that way in the German Army. In time, von Braun would find himself drawn into a web of politics, warfare, and internal intrigue. He would find himself building weapons of war for one of the most truly evil leaders of modern times. He would be arrested for suspected espionage, nearly killed in an Allied bomber raid, and build rockets that would fly to the edge of outer space. And all of this by the time he was thirty-three years old.

But, in the early 1930s, all of these events were still far in the future . . .

In the army, von Braun learned the intricacies of dealing with a bureaucracy, yet another lesson that would stand him in good stead in later years. Whenever a team of engineers needed equipment, it was necessary to fill out multiple requisition forms and pass them through the required channels. Although the team was given priority in receiving rocket parts and scientific equipment, they found it virtually impossible to obtain the simple office equipment—pencils and typewriters— that they needed to take care of their paperwork; they had not been given a budget for such items by the powers that be. Then they discovered that they could obtain such equipment quite easily through a simple trick— make it sound as if they were ordering scientific instruments and rocket parts!

"Even the keenest Budget Bureau official," Dornberger later wrote, "could not suspect that 'Appliance for milling wooden dowels up to 10 millimeters in diameter, as per sample' meant a pencil sharpener, or that 'Instrument for recording test data with rotating roller as per sample' meant a typewriter. . . . And if there was nothing else to do, we entrenched ourselves behind the magic word 'secret.' There the Budget Bureau was powerless."[11]

Von Braun built his first rocket for the army in the fall of 1932; more precisely, he built a rocket engine, the part of the rocket where the fuel is burned and thrust is produced. The rocket engine was given its first static test on December 21, 1932, a memorable occasion that Walter Dornberger would later recall quite vividly in his book *V-2*. The rocket engine was mounted on a brand-new test stand at the Experimental Station West. Von Braun ignited the engine by setting fire to a can of gasoline on the end of a 12-foot (3.6-m) rod and holding it under the rocket's exhaust nozzle, while Dornberger and other observers took cover behind nearby trees.

" 'Cover' was an optimistic term," Dornberger wrote. "It could hardly be expected that the slender fir trunk 4 inches thick would provide much protection against an explosion."[12]

The rocket engine roared to life. And then . . .

> There was a swoosh, a hiss, and—crash!
> Clouds of smoke rose. A single flame darted briefly upward and vanished. Cables, boards, metal sheeting, fragments of steel and aluminum flew whistling through the air. The searchlights went out.
> Silence.
> In the suddenly darkened pit of the testing room a milky, slimy mixture of alcohol and oxygen burned spasmodically with flames of different shapes and sizes, occasionally crackling and detonating like fireworks. Steam hissed. Cables were on fire in a hundred places. Thick, black, stinging fumes of burning rubber filled the air. Von Braun and I stared at each other wide-eyed. We were uninjured.[13]

It was an inauspicious debut for a young man who would one day be in the top ranks of rocket scientists. In a sense, however, the experiment was successful. Von Braun and Dornberger quickly realized where they had gone wrong and set about to correct the error. But as Dornberger later noted: "Alas, that winter's night of 1932 we could not foresee how many more fundamental errors we were to fall into before success gradually rewarded our efforts many years later."[14]

Experiments on rocket engines and other parts proceeded apace at Kummersdorf, until in 1933 it was decided that it was time to build a complete rocket. Since the rocket would be an "aggregate" of the various parts then undergoing testing, it was dubbed *Aggregate-1, A-1* for short. The *A-1* was to have a thrust of 300 kilograms. The combustion chamber where the fuel was to be burned—the *engine*, in rocket terminology—would be built into the middle of the fuel tank, so that the liquid fuel could cool the chamber from the outside and keep it from vaporizing under the intense heat of the burning fuel.

The main problem to be solved in building the *A-1* was that of stability. How were they to keep the rocket from veering wildly out of control, as so many of the VfR's rockets were prone to do?

Dornberger was a former artilleryman. He knew that bullets and other projectiles were given a "spin" as they were fired so that they rotated during flight; this rotation kept them stable, in the same way that rotation keeps a gyroscope stable.

A rocket with spin would be more stable than a rocket that didn't spin, but centrifugal force would cause the fuel to slosh around the walls of the fuel tank, making it difficult to pump fuel into the engine. Hence, the *A-1* was designed so that only the top part, a heavy steel cylinder, rotated; this part of the rocket was called, naturally enough, the gyroscope. In theory, the gyroscope would keep the *A-1* on course during flight, but before it was built, the Kummersdorf engineers realized that the *A-1*'s gyroscope was in the wrong place. It had to be in the middle of the rocket. According to their calculations, a rocket with a gyroscope on its nose could never be truly stable.

Plans for the *A-1* rocket were scrapped. A new rocket was designed, which Dornberger and von Braun dubbed the *A-2*. Unlike the *A-1*, the *A-2* was actually built. In early December 1934, two *A-2* rockets were taken by the Kummersdorf team to an island in the North Sea called Borkum. The two rockets had been affectionately named "Max" and "Moritz," after characters in a popular German comic strip. (The same strip appeared in the United States as "The Katzenjammer Kids," though the characters were renamed Hans and Fritz, possibly the only German first names with which Americans of the period were familiar.)

the *A-2* rocket in its test stand, 1935

The rocket firings were successful. One of the rockets attained a record height of 1.4 miles (2.2 km). The Kummersdorf team had made a breakthrough. Now they began dreaming of larger and larger rockets. Although their ostensible goal was to build rockets that would carry bombs over long distances, most of the Kummersdorf engineers—and especially Wernher von Braun—had a very different goal in mind: they wanted to build rockets that would fly into outer space, rockets that would carry human beings to the moon and beyond.

But to build rockets larger than Max and Moritz, even to build larger missiles, required one thing that von Braun and his fellow engineers were perpetually short of—money. Then, in January 1935, a large sum of cash fell into the Kummersdorf team's lap.

In that month Major Wolfram Von Richtofen, cousin of the famous World War I flying ace, visited the Experimental Station West to watch a demonstration of the rocket engines the team had built. Von Richtofen was an officer in the newly formed German Air Force known as the *Luftwaffe.* He was particularly interested in developing a new type of airplane, the jet, and he felt that the rocket work at Kummersdorf might lead to the development of rocketlike engines for airplanes.

Von Richtofen was so impressed by what he saw at Kummersdorf that he offered the rocket engineers 5 million *reichsmarks* to further their research. Excited by the offer but not sure if he was allowed to accept funds from the air force, Dornberger went immediately to his superior, General Becker, who was now Chief of Ordnance. Becker replied angrily, "Just like that upstart *Luftwaffe!* No sooner do we come up with a promising development than they try to pinch it! But they'll find that they're the junior partners in the rocket business!"

Colonel Ritter Von Horstig, one of the officers at

Kummersdorf, looked at Becker with surprise. "Do you mean that you propose to spend more than five million on rocketry?"

"Exactly that," retorted Becker. "I intend to appropriate six million on top of Von Richtofen's five!"[15]

The Kummersdorf team now had the money it needed to build bigger and better rockets. But it would need a place to test them. Kummersdorf was already too small; it had been necessary to fire the *A-2* on an island in the North Sea, and the engineers could hardly be expected to pack up and travel to the seaside every time they had a rocket to launch. Further, they would need larger facilities for an enlarged staff, and a place to build and test the large rockets.

Ideally, they needed a place remote from cities and houses, preferably by the sea, where stray rockets could crash into the ocean rather than populated neighborhoods. Von Braun and Dornberger looked for such a place with little success—at first. Von Braun found an ideal location on a Baltic Sea island called Rugen, but a Nazi organization called "Strength Through Joy" had seen it first and turned it into a recreation area. Then, in December 1935, von Braun found the very place that he had sought, a town with a name that would become legendary in the history of rocketry: Peenemünde.

Like Dorothy's land over the rainbow, it had been right in von Braun's backyard all along, figuratively speaking. While visiting his mother over the Christmas holiday, he mentioned the search for a rocket test site. His mother recalled that her father had once hunted ducks on the Baltic island of Usedom. It had been remote and quite beautiful. Perhaps Wernher should take a look.

Von Braun did, and found paradise. The island was an unspoiled wilderness, sparsely populated and far from the hub of civilization. The town of Peenemünde lay on the north shore of the island, where the river

Peene emptied into the Baltic; the name Peenemünde means, in fact, "mouth of the Peene." Just north of Usedom and above Peenemünde was a smaller island, called the Griefswalder Oie, a perfect spot for launching rockets. There was a small inn on the island, where the rocket engineers could refresh themselves after a long day of testing; the main facilities could be placed at Peenemünde.

As von Braun, an amateur sailor and enthusiastic outdoorsman, later said: "It was love at first sight. Marvelous sailing!"[16]

Von Braun brought word of his find to Dornberger and encouraged him to take a look. Dornberger was just as impressed with the island as von Braun had been and arranged for the land to be purchased and facilities constructed there. Meanwhile, the team settled down to design and build a new, larger rocket, which they called the *A-3*. But even as the *A-3* was on the drawing board, they turned their restless and inventive minds to bigger things.

If the *A-3* worked successfully, von Braun and Dornberger reasoned, it would then be time to build a *real* rocket, one that could serve as the first real war rocket since the British had abandoned rocketry in the nineteenth century—and, not incidentally, a rocket that could fly to the very edge of outer space and beyond.

This rocket would be called the *A-4*. Though they had no way of knowing it at the time, this was the rocket that would go down in history as the *V-2*. It would be the progenitor of present-day ICBMs, but it would also be the progenitor of the rockets that would launch astronauts to the moon.

What would the *A-4* be like? In order to compete with conventional artillery, Dornberger knew that the *A-4* would need a range at least twice that of the largest gun ever built, the Paris Gun. Since the range of the Paris Gun had been 80 miles (125 km), the *A-4* needed to have a range of 160 miles (256 km). And it needed to be able to fire a larger bomb than the Paris Gun; this wasn't difficult, since the Paris Gun was capable of firing only a small projectile. In addition, both men knew that the *A-4* would be capable of flying through outer space on the way to its target; this was the feature that most excited von Braun. In time, he hoped that he could convince the German government to turn this war rocket into a space rocket.

While the *A-3* was being built, the rocket team from Kummersdorf moved to Peenemünde. The staff had now swelled to ninety persons. The new equipment included a giant wind tunnel, which von Braun had requested. The wind tunnel allowed the engineers to test their rockets at simulated supersonic velocities before they were even fired, so that problems of stability could, with luck, be spotted while the rocket was still being put together.

Shortly after the move to Peenemünde, the *A-3* was ready for testing. The results were disastrous.

The *A-3* never worked. It was the first rocket to be fired from the new launching pad on the island of Greifswalder Oie, in December 1937, and none of its firings went as expected. However, this was not an omen of the rocket team's future at Peenemünde.

The *A-3* was a much larger rocket than any von Braun and his team had built before. It was more than 21 feet (6.3 m) tall and 2 feet (0.6 m) thick. It was to have a thrust of 3,000 pounds (1,350 kg) or more. In flight, it would be controlled by special vanes—that is, fins— inside the exhaust nozzle. These vanes would control the angle at which the hot exhaust emerged from the nozzle and could be used to change the direction of the rocket's flight. Vanes on the outside of the rocket could be used in the same way but would only work if the rocket were flying through air, which might not always be the case. For testing purposes, the *A-3* was equipped with a parachute, which would open at the top of the rocket's trajectory—that is, at the highest point in its flight—so that the rocket could float harmlessly back to earth and be retrieved for future tests.

Troubles began at the first firing. The rocket tilted into the wind, opened its parachute, and crashed into the ocean. On the second firing, the same thing happened. Afraid that the parachute itself might have caused the problem, they removed it. After a hiatus of several days, during which the Greifswalder Oie was locked in fog, another *A-3* was fired. Once again, the rocket turned into the wind and dropped into the sea. Could the wind itself have caused the problem? Some quick calculations showed that it probably had; the *A-3* couldn't fly in even a mild crosswind. Von Braun later wrote: "While the power plant [the engine] behaved as expected, the guidance and control system was a flop in all three firings."[17]

In frustration, the *A-3* was scrapped and plans were made to design yet another rocket. But what to call it? The name *A-4* had already been reserved for the BIG rocket, the one that would fly to the edge of space and deliver bombs over a range twice that of the Paris Gun. And the name *A-3* had become associated with disaster. Thus, the next rocket was dubbed *A-5*.

The engine of the *A-3*, perhaps the only part of the earlier rocket that had performed properly, was moved intact to the *A-5*, but the hull was given a brand-new shape, which, as it turned out, would be identical to that in the *A-4* super-rocket. New vanes and a new system for controlling the rocket's flight were installed.

As von Braun wrote: "The first *A-5* was launched, still with no control [system], in the fall of 1938. One year later . . . the first *A-5* with all the trimmings took off and performed a flawless vertical flight to an altitude of 12 kilometers, say 7-½ miles."[18]

The *A-5* was a success! Now von Braun's team could

turn their attention to building a *real* rocket, not just a test rocket but a rocket that would not only be the ultimate war weapon but the first rocket capable of flying into outer space.

But while the *A-5* was being tested, an event of monumental significance occurred, one that would determine not only the future of von Braun and his rocket team but the future of the entire world.

World War II began.

3 "We have invaded space with our rocket . . ."

Adolf Hitler never made a secret of his desire to reclaim the portions of Germany lost after World War I. When Hitler showed signs of a dangerous belligerence in the late 1930s, the leaders of certain European nations believed that they could "appease" him by offering him a few pieces of Czechoslovakia that had earlier belonged to Germany, but they were wrong. Hitler wanted it all . . . and then some.

In the mid-1930s, Hitler blatantly disregarded the Treaty of Versailles and built the army back to its full strength. In the fall of 1939, after signing a treaty with the Soviet Union, Hitler felt strong enough to risk a potential world war and attacked Poland, which held some of the territories that had belonged to Germany before the First World War.

Poland had allies that should have come to its rescue and probably would have, except for one thing. Hitler was engaged in a new kind of war: the *Blitzkrieg*, or "lightning war." He rolled into Poland with masses of tanks and troops and attacked with such blinding speed that the battle was over before Poland's potential saviors could decide what response they ought to make.

The rest of the world was left to wonder if Hitler would be satisfied with merely conquering Poland. He wasn't. In 1940, he moved again, capturing Norway,

Denmark, and, finally, France. Encouraged by his success and unsated by the capture of lands that had once
belonged to Germany, he moved to conquer the rest
of Europe. And so began World War II.

This put von Braun and his team of rocket engineers
in a new position. No longer were they building potential weapons for a nation at peace; they were building
very real weapons for a nation at war. Did this mean
the Peenemünde team would receive large sums of
money to build rockets so that they could be used to
wage war on Germany's enemies, the so-called Allies?
(Germany and the nations with which it was allied—
primarily Italy and Japan—were called the Axis powers.) As it turned out, Hitler saw no use at all for rockets. His *Blitzkrieg* strategy, organized primarily around
tanks, was wildly successful, and for long-range bombardment, he had a fleet of airplanes, flown by the
Luftwaffe. Why risk money on a new and untried technology when that same money could be better spent on
conventional weapons? This may have been a mistake
on Hitler's part, but it was a very fortunate mistake for
the world at large. If the work at Peenemünde had
proceeded faster than it did, the outcome of the war
might have been quite different—and the world today
would be a very different place.

Early in 1939, von Braun got a first-hand glimpse of the
man who would soon plunge the world into war, when
Hitler himself visited Peenemünde.

The rocket team had entertained a number of high-
powered visitors in the past, both from other branches
of the armed services and from the Nazi hierarchy. They
knew how to impress these visitors: fire off a few large
rocket motors and have the charming and articulate von
Braun explain what made them function. It had worked
with Von Richtofen, and it had worked with any number of minor officials.

But it didn't work with Hitler.

The *Fuhrer* arrived in March 1939, only a few months before his invasion of Poland, accompanied by a pair of officials. Dornberger met him on arrival at Kummersdorf West. (Not all of the facilities had yet been moved to Peenemünde, and Hitler doubtlessly preferred the short drive to the suburbs of Berlin.) Dornberger later wrote: "I immediately had the impression that his thoughts were elsewhere. As he shook hands with me his eyes seemed to look through me to something beyond. His remarkably tanned face, with the unsightly snub nose, little black moustache, and extremely thin lips, showed no sort of interest in what we were to show him."[19]

Von Braun, who had been warned by Dornberger not to talk about his dreams of spaceflight in front of the *Fuhrer*, fell in with the party and accompanied Hitler through a series of rocket demonstrations, explaining the results when the opportunity arose. Hitler watched the demonstrations in silence. First, an old rocket motor was given a static test, then a larger engine, with more than 2,000 pounds (907 kg) of thrust, was fired. The noise was deafening, but Hitler was unimpressed.

Finally, Hitler was shown a newly constructed *A-5* rocket, the largest rocket yet built by the team. Von Braun explained its construction and operation in detail while Hitler watched. The *Fuhrer* asked a few perfunctory questions. As he listened, von Braun became aware that Hitler had absolutely no knowledge of rocketry whatsoever. Perhaps this should not have been surprising, but von Braun was embarrassed to find himself in the position of explaining the most elementary laws of action/reaction and ballistic flight to the supreme dictator of the land. Cautiously, he told Hitler why rockets would be preferable to other forms of long-range weapons, why they required esoteric and previously untried fuel systems, and so forth. Hitler listened quietly, displaying interest only when von Braun discussed the ability of rockets larger than the *A-5* to carry substantial payloads, such as explosive warheads.

Later, as the engineers and their visitors finished lunch at the mess hall, Hitler raised his glass of mineral water in a polite toast. *"Es war doch gewaltig!"* he said. (Roughly translated: "Well, it was grand!") This was the closest thing to a complimentary remark that the dictator had made all day, and it was taken by the Peenemünde engineers as damning with faint praise. On that note, the dictator left.

Dornberger was angered by Hitler's behavior. "I simply could not understand why this man, who always showed the greatest interest in all new weapons, who found no gun or tank too difficult, who when new guns were demonstrated could hardly be induced to leave and wanted all technical details explained, had shown no sign of enthusiasm on his visit to us. Why that brain, equipped, so far as all questions of armament were concerned, with a positively staggering memory for figures, could not take in the true significance of our rockets remained a mystery to me."[20]

As it turned out, Dornberger and von Braun would meet Hitler again, just a few years later, under very different circumstances. And his response to their rocket demonstrations would be *very* different.

But by then the war would be on a very different course. And the rocket engineers would have completed the *A-4* . . .

In the intervening period, a number of von Braun's fellow rocketeers from the VfR had joined him in working for the army. The most notable of these was Hermann Oberth, whose theories had made the army's rockets possible. But Oberth played only a minor role at Peenemünde. Another who went to work at Peenemünde was von Braun's younger brother, Magnus.

There was a general feeling at Peenemünde that Rudolf Nebel also deserved some form of thanks for the tireless work he had performed with the VfR, but no one wanted to hire him as an engineer. Instead, the army arranged to pay Nebel for the rights to one of his rocket designs, which they then filed away and never used.

In the years after the beginning of World War II, the Peenemünde project was kept alive by Field-Marshal Walther von Brauschitsch, who for a time was Supreme Commander of the German Army. Von Brauschitsch had been deeply impressed by the work that von Braun and the others were doing, as Hitler had not been. He arranged for more than 3,500 soldiers and officers to be transferred to Peenemünde, where they were put to work building rockets.

In a moment of inspiration, von Braun arranged for a special conference of scientists to be held at Peenemünde, which he called "Wisdom Day." The purpose of Wisdom Day was to appropriate some free help from the academic community and, in an odd sort of way, to subvert the Nazis. Or so von Braun recalled, years after the fact:

> Since the universities were also suffering from conscription, the professors were all the more eager to participate in a novel scientific effort which might also place academics in better rapport with the government. Very willingly, each returned to his institute or university with one or more problems in his briefcase, the tasks having been selected by the professors themselves, in accordance with the facilities available to them. Problems thus farmed out included integrating accelerometers, improvement of pump impellers, trajectory tracking by Doppler radio, gyroscope bearings, research on radio wave propagation in the ionosphere antenna patterns, new measuring methods for our supersonic wind tunnel,

computing machines for flight mechanics and many others. . . .

The arrangement between Peenemünde and these 36 professors withstood a later attempt of the Nazis to "organize" all wartime research in Germany. When loud-mouthed and heavy-handed party men presented lists and forms to be filled in by the universities, those working with us would politely decline to cooperate, pointing out that they were fully occupied with high-priority work for Peenemünde.[21]

The *A-4* rocket took roughly four years to build, from 1939 to 1942. During that period, funding for the army's rockets came and went as Hitler's fortunes waxed and waned. The rocket team and Peenemünde were never exactly flooded with money during that period, but with the help of Field-Marshal von Brauschitsch they made do. Dornberger periodically went off to the government with hat in hand on what he termed "begging expeditions," to ask for more money. Somehow, the rocket was built.

On June 13, 1942, the *A-4* was ready to fly. It was placed on the test pad, ignited, rose a few feet into the air, and crumpled back onto the launching pad. It then exploded in a huge ball of fire.

The second *A-4*, launched on August 16, 1942, performed somewhat better, but only somewhat. It flew for forty-five seconds, reaching a considerable altitude, then broke apart. Apparently, the skin of the rocket was too weak to withstand the stresses to which it had been subjected. The *A-4* was redesigned accordingly.

Von Braun and Dornberger knew that if they were to receive more money for building rockets, they were going to have to make the *A-4* fly. And if they didn't make it fly on its next test, they might not have another chance. On October 3, 1942, they prepared yet another *A-4* for a test launching and crossed their fingers.

Hundreds of technicians and visitors stood by for the

launch. Cameras were trained on the 13.5-ton rocket to capture its flight—if, indeed, it flew. Von Braun held his breath in fear that this flight would fail as the others had. He and Dornberger, along with a group of engineers, watched from a nearby rooftop.

As the moment of launch approached, the Peenemünde engineers went through a ritual that had become common at the Griefswalder Oie launching site. They recited a countdown. "X minus 3," shouted one of the engineers through a loudspeaker when three minutes remained before firing. "Counting off."

The countdown would later become a familiar ritual. Indeed, it would become a cliché of the Space Age during the many televised launchings at Cape Canaveral in the United States. Some historians date the idea of the countdown to the movie *Frau im Mond*, for which Oberth had earlier attempted to build a rocket. According to an essay that von Braun wrote in the 1960s, it was intended to help the engineers organize the process of readying the rocket and to give bystanders plenty of time to get out of the way.

Finally, the word that the observers had been waiting for boomed out of the loudspeaker: "Ignition!" The huge *A-4* engines roared to life. Clouds of smoke, filled with sparks, gushed out of the nozzle at the bottom of the *A-4*. Then the smoke filled with flame and the rocket rose into the air on 25 tons of thrust.

A solid wall of noise struck the onlookers. The rocket flew almost straight upward in perfect flight. As it dwindled into the sky the observers raised binoculars to their eyes to follow it. Then the rocket tilted toward the east, as planned.

Only five seconds had passed since the rocket was launched, though to the engineers on the ground those five seconds must have seemed like an eternity.

The voice from the loudspeaker counted off the seconds of the rocket's flight. At approximately twenty-five seconds, the rocket passed the speed of sound. Although the engineers had feared that this milestone might prove deadly to the rocket, it continued flying.

Then, at forty seconds, the rocket nearly disappeared in a cloud of white smoke. Had it exploded? No, explained the voice on the loudspeaker. The oxygen vent had opened. Water vapor filled the air. The rocket left a strange, jagged vapor trail behind it, whipped by the wildly varying air currents that the rocket was passing through, a phenomenon that the engineers later came to call "frozen lightning."

At fifty-four seconds came the moment that the engineers called *brenschluss*—the cutoff of the rocket engines. Now the rocket was coasting on its own momentum. It was a ballistic projectile, a giant bullet, coasting through the fringes of outer space.

Von Braun and Dornberger, who had been watching from a distance, rushed to a nearby automobile and drove to Test Stand VII, where the rest of the engineers were rejoicing in what Dornberger described as "something like a popular riot."[22] The launching area was scorched and in disarray; mooring cables hung loose from platforms. But in the middle of this chaos the rocket engineers were cheering wildly, shaking one another's hands.

Finally, at 296 seconds—nearly five minutes—after launching, the rocket fell back to earth. The radio signal that the rocket had broadcast back to the Griefswalder Oie throughout its flight suddenly ceased. As Dornberger described it: "The rocket had struck the Earth with an impact energy of 1,400 million foot-pounds, corresponding to that of 50 express engines each weighing 100 tons and all racing along together at 60 mph [97 kmph]."[23]

Later that evening, Dornberger gave a speech that summed up the events of the day:

[F]or the first time a machine of human construction, a 5.5-ton missile, covered a distance of 120 miles [193 km] with a lateral deflection [i.e., bad aim] of only 2-½ miles [4 km] from the target. . . .

We are the first to have given a rocket built on the principles of aircraft construction a speed of 3,300 mph [5,310 kmph] by means of the jet drive peculiar to rockets. . . . We have thus proved that it is quite possible to build piloted missiles or aircraft to fly at supersonic speed, given the right form and suitable propulsion. Our self-steering rocket has reached heights never touched by a man-made machine. . . . our rocket today reached a height of nearly 60 miles [97 km]. We have thus broken the height record of 25 miles [40 km] previously held by the shell fired from the now almost legendary Paris Gun. . . .

We have invaded space with our rocket and for the first time—mark this well—have used space as a bridge between two points on the earth; we have proved rocket propulsion practicable for space travel. To land, sea, and air may now be added infinite space as a medium of future intercontinental traffic. This third day of October, 1942, is the first of a new era of transportation, that of space travel.[24]

It was, as Dornberger recognized, the dawn of the Space Age. But it was also the dawn of another, darker era: the age of the missile. The *A-4* was the direct ancestor of the missiles that in a later era would sit in silos on both sides of the world waiting to carry nuclear weapons from one continent to another. Appropriately enough, it was born in a time of war.

4 "Fire, everywhere fire!"

After the phenomenal success of the third *A-4* test, you might think that the rocket engineers would have little trouble securing funds to build more rockets. But in late 1942 and early 1943, all was not well at Peenemünde.

Field-Marshal von Brauchitsch, whose influence had kept the rocket project afloat through hard times, had been dismissed. General Becker, who had been head of the Army Weapons Department when rocket development had begun, had committed suicide after an argument with Hitler. The upper echelons of the Third Reich looked askance at the money being wasted on rockets.

Worse, the Peenemünde team now had competition. The air force was building its own missile, the *Fi-103*. Actually, the *Fi-103* was a robot jet plane, which could carry bombs on unmanned "suicide" missions, an ancestor of the modern cruise missile. Later, it would be renamed the *Vergeltungswaffe Ein*—the *Vengeance Weapon One, V-1* for short. It would be used in the bombardment of England, where it would be nicknamed the "buzz bomb" or "doodlebug." The *V-1* siphoned away development money from the *A-4*, and for a time threatened to scuttle the Peenemünde project completely.

Albert Speer, Hitler's chief architect and minister in charge of war production, promoted von Braun's cause and once saved him from possible execution.

Worst of all, Hitler himself had dreamed—literally— that no *A-4* rocket would ever bombard England, the preferred target for the new missile. Hitler was a great believer in omens. For von Braun and his rocket builders, Hitler's dream was a bad omen indeed.

Nonetheless, the rocket team still had friends in the Third Reich. Perhaps the most notable was Albert Speer, Hitler's minister of armaments. Many years later, in his autobiographical book *Inside the Third Reich*, Speer wrote of von Braun and the others:

Ever since the winter of 1939, I had been closely associated with the Peenemünde development center, although at first all I was doing was meeting its construction needs. [Speer was also Hitler's official architect.] I liked mingling with this circle of non-political young scientists and inventors headed by Wernher von Braun, twenty-seven years old, purposeful, a man realistically at home in the future. Under the somewhat paternalistic direction of Colonel Walter Dornberger these young men were able to work unhampered by bureaucratic obstacles and pursue ideas which at times sounded thoroughly utopian.

The work, mere glimmerings of which were sketched out in 1939, also exerted a strange fascination upon me. It was like the planning of a miracle. I was impressed anew by these technicians with their fantastic visions, these mathematical romantics. Whenever I visited Peenemünde I also felt, quite spontaneously, somewhat akin to them. My sympathy stood them in good stead when in the late fall of 1939 Hitler crossed the rocket project off his list of urgent undertakings and thus automatically cut off its labor and materials. By tacit agreement with the Army Ordnance Office, I continued to build the Peenemünde installations without its approval—a liberty that probably no one but myself could have taken.

After my appointment as Minister of Armaments, I naturally took a keener interest in the project. Hitler, however, continued to be exceedingly skeptical. He was filled with a fundamental distrust of all innovations

61

which, as in the case of jet aircraft or atom bombs, went beyond the technical experience of the First World War generation and presaged an era he could not know.[25]

In July 1943, Hitler's skepticism vanished. The rocket team was given top priority. Suddenly everyone wanted to be involved with rocket production. Supplies arrived by the truckload.

What had happened? What was different now?

A lot, as it turned out. The war was not going well for Hitler. Although few in Germany were aware of it, he had bitten off more than he could chew. In the early months of the war, Hitler had chosen his targets carefully, striking at one or two nations at a time, invading with such relentless force and speed that the Allies had had no time to organize a concerted defense against him.

But things had begun to go wrong. England had refused to be conquered, and Hitler had been forced to expend much energy—particularly on the part of the *Luftwaffe*, which fought desperate air battles over the English Channel and England itself—in an unsuccessful attempt to subjugate that nation. Foolishly, Hitler had attacked Russia, with which he had earlier signed a nonintervention treaty, and had brought down the wrath of that giant nation. And finally, Hitler had made a sufficient nuisance of himself in Europe that the most powerful nation of all, the United States, had joined in the war against him. The German Army may have been one of the great fighting machines of the twentieth century, but now it was hopelessly outnumbered and outgunned.

Hitler was desperate. And suddenly the *A-4*, a brand-new weapon with possibly fantastic capabilities, seemed like the answer to his prayers.

On July 7, von Braun and Dornberger were summoned to Hitler's headquarters. They hastily put together a collection of materials—film, scale models, drawings, charts, everything they could find—to show Hitler how the work was progressing at Peenemünde. The leader of the Third Reich welcomed them with open arms. It was the first time in four years that the engineers had seen Hitler. They were startled by the changes in him. He seemed older, tired, his face pallid, his shoulders bent. He was obviously a man under great pressure, a man who was beginning to understand that he was going to lose the battle that he had started.

"*Der Fuhrer* looked much older, and he was wearing his first pair of glasses," von Braun said later. "But when we described our accomplishments to him, his face lighted with enthusiasm."[26]

They showed him a movie while von Braun narrated. The film depicted a series of *A-4* tests, mixing live and animated sequences of the rocket's flight. At the end, the words "We made it after all!" appeared on the screen.

When the lights came up, Hitler stared at the blank screen in silence, his features flushed with emotion. Finally, Dornberger broke the awkward silence with a speech about the *A-4* and its capabilities. Hitler listened with great interest. When Dornberger finished speaking, Hitler rose and shook his hand. The *Fuhrer* spoke in a hoarse whisper: "I thank you. Why was it I could not believe in the success of your work? If we had had these rockets in 1939, we should never have had this war. . . . Europe and the world will be too small from now on to contain a war. With such weapons humanity will be unable to endure it."[27]

If Hitler was more impressed this time around with the work of the rocket team, von Braun was also more impressed with Hitler than he had been during their first meeting.

"I began to see the shape of the man," he said later, "his brilliance, the tremendous force of his personality. It gripped you somehow. But also you could see his

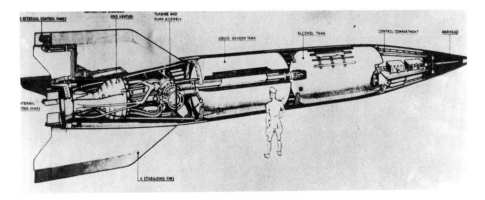

a diagram of the *A-4* (later renamed *V-2*)

flaw—he was wholly without scruples, a godless man who thought himself the only god, the only authority he needed."[28]

Hitler was tremendously enthusiastic about the new rocket, so enthusiastic that he ordered the Peenemünde team to produce huge quantities of them—2,000 a month. The engineers, amazed by this request, informed Hitler that the rocket was still in the experimental stage and could not possibly be produced in such quantities. The *Fuhrer* would not be dissuaded. Furthermore, he wanted the *A-4* to carry a 10-ton bomb as payload and refused to believe the engineers when they told him that this was physically impossible.

Hitler saw the rocket as a miracle weapon. It would win the war that he had begun to believe he could not win. It was a beacon of hope in his moment of despair.

And, in fact, the *A-4* was indeed a miracle, a miracle of technology. But even miracles need time to grow, to develop, to be brought to fruition. Hitler wasn't willing to give it that time. Hard-pressed to maintain Germany's war effort against an opposition that seemed to grow in strength and ferocity every day, he wasn't *able* to give it time. The *A-4* was to be put into mass production immediately and readied for the bombardment of England and other targets in Western Europe.

The age of the missile had begun—just a little prematurely.

The obvious place to build the *A-4* missiles was at Peenemünde, with its wonderfully isolated wilderness location. But Peenemünde wasn't as safely isolated as it seemed.

By 1943, the Allies had begun to harbor suspicions about this tiny installation on the Baltic Sea. Aerial reconnaissance photographs showed peculiar activities there. Strange flying devices had been spotted in the vicinity, occasionally whizzing along the coastlines of neighboring countries.

On August 17, 1943, von Braun awoke in the middle of the night to the sound of explosions echoing in the distance. Had something gone wrong with the rockets? Had some improperly stored fuel caught fire and led to an explosion? Dornberger, sleeping in a nearby building, later recalled that he at first thought that unauthorized rocket testing was being performed in the middle of the night and only realized that something was wrong when the sounds—a sharp S-s-st—bang! S-s-st—bang!—continued incessantly. When Dornberger raced outside he found von Braun and another man already stumbling through the darkness toward a concrete shelter. A strange, smoky mist filled the air.

"I suppose you forgot all about me!" Dornberger chided.

"No," replied von Braun. "We were just coming to get you."

The sound of explosions echoed between the buildings. Airplanes droned through the darkness above. Anti-aircraft guns chattered in the distance.

"What the devil's it all about?" Dornberger asked. "Ten to one the AA [anti-aircraft installations] were too keen and brought this down on us."

"No, no!" shouted von Braun. "This time they're really going for us!"[29]

Inside the shelter, they phoned the Peenemünde army command post and were told that a flight of Allied bombers was passing overhead. Apparently the bombers were aiming at the rocket test stands, but so far none had been hit. Several workshops were burning, though, and the power station was out. Von Braun and Dornberger rushed back out into the night, hoping to find some way to deal with the emergency.

Dornberger shouted urgent orders: "Von Braun, you will take over the construction bureau with all the men in the shelter and the Air Force construction labor gang. Try to restrict the fire to the top floor. Get a hose from the fire brigade."[30]

Von Braun nodded his acknowledgment and raced toward Building 4, where the construction labor gang was housed. He arrived to find a scene of terrible chaos. One of his secretaries, Hannelore Bannasch, wrote a vivid account of what followed in her diary:

> Haus [building] 4 burns brightly. Haus 5 is in flames. Everywhere I look it's fire. Fire, everywhere fire—horrible beauty! We run past a building completely burnt. Here and there it still crackles. . . . Even the shrubbery is on fire. . . . My hair singes.
>
> I am frightened back, I cannot go through a pool of blood in front of me. In it lies a leg torn from a body still in a military trouser leg and boot.
>
> There is my professor [von Braun]! We must save the secret documents!
>
> But the building is burning. The roof is already down. The gable is ready to fall at any moment. The second story is gone. Can we risk the stairs? The professor takes my hand, quickly and cautiously. There is a roaring, crashing, and crackling.
>
> Groping along the wall we reach the second floor: one, two, three, four, five—yes, this was our door. We must go in there! There are no more doors here now. Fire is to the left and in front of us. We press ourselves

tightly against the still standing wall. The other half of the room has collapsed.

We are now in the room. Out with the safe and out with the other furnishings! I run up and down the stairs with the secret papers as long as I am able. The professor is still upstairs with a few men. They throw things that are still usable out of the window. Down below, I gather things together, put them into the upturned safe.

The heat is dreadful. A soldier comes and stands by the safe with his rifle loaded. Slowly, dawn breaks. I return to the air raid shelter. The secret papers are secure.[31]

In the light of dawn the extent of the damage became obvious. Seven hundred and thirty-five people were dead, including two of the chief engineers. From the air, Peenemünde looked as if it had been built on the cratered surface of the moon; gaping holes were scattered along the ground where bombs had struck. And yet, surprisingly, Peenemünde was not so badly damaged that research work could not proceed there. But it was decided immediately after the raid that the damage inflicted by the Allies during the raid would *not* be repaired, so that it would appear from the air that the installation had been successfully knocked out of commission. To repair the damage would be to invite another raid even worse than the first.

It was obvious now that the Allies knew about Peenemünde and at least suspected what was being developed there. This meant that Peenemünde would be useless as a site for building the *A-4* rockets. Instead, a major factory was set up in the Harz Mountains, near the city of Nordhausen. It was given the name *Mittelwerk*—literally, "middle works." The huge factory was actually located inside a mountain, so that it would be safe from spying airplanes and bombing raids like the one that had hit Peenemünde.

Mittelwerk remains to this day one of the blackest episodes in the history of rocketry. It was located near the Dora concentration camp, and inmates from the camp were put to work building rockets in the factory. They were literally worked to death—fed barely enough food to keep them alive, beaten, and even murdered if they performed inadequately, allowed to collapse and die when they could work no more. Von Braun, who occasionally visited the factory, was certainly aware of the inhuman conditions under which the laborers were worked, but he did nothing about it. Perhaps there was nothing that he could do.

Hitler's enthusiasm over the *A-4* had a number of results at Peenemünde. Von Braun was given the honorary title of professor. The *A-4* was given the new name *Vergeltungswaffe Zwei*—Vengeance Weapon Two, after the earlier naming of the *Fi-103* missile—*V-2* for short. This was the name by which the world would soon know it, and by which history would remember it.

Now that the rocket had been given Hitler's blessing, a number of figures in the Nazi hierarchy were interested in cutting themselves a piece of the pie. Most prominent among these opportunistic individuals was Heinrich Himmler, head of Hitler's fearsome secret police agency, the *Gestapo*. Himmler wanted to control the rocket project, and he was willing to use unscrupulous means to achieve his goal.

In February 1944, von Braun was summoned to Himmler's office. Himmler, whom von Braun would later describe as "as mild-mannered a villain as ever cut a throat,"[32] greeted von Braun politely, then offered the engineer his sales pitch.

"I hope you realize," Himmler said, "that your *A-4* rocket has ceased to be a toy and that the whole German people eagerly await the mystery weapon. . . . As for you, I can imagine that you've been immensely handicapped by army red tape. Why not join my staff? Surely you know that no one has such ready access to *der Fuhrer*, and I promise you vastly more effective support than can those hidebound generals. . . ."

Von Braun wanted nothing to do with Himmler. And the last thing in the world he was likely to do was leave the army to work for the *Gestapo*. But he also realized that the powerful and vindictive Himmler must be handled with diplomacy. Delicately, he replied: *"Herr Reichsfuhrer, I couldn't ask for a better chief than General Dornberger. Such delays as we're still experiencing are due to technical troubles and not to red tape. You know, the V-2 is rather like a little flower. In order to flourish, it needs sunshine, a well-proportioned quantity of fertilizer, and a gentle gardener. What I fear you're planning is a big jet of liquid manure! You know, that might kill our little flower."*[33]

Himmler, unconvinced by this speech, dismissed von Braun from his office. Von Braun, on the other hand, tried to dismiss the incident from his mind, but a few days later he received a forcible reminder. At two o'clock one morning he woke to a loud hammering on his door. Three agents from the *Gestapo* stood outside. They arrested von Braun and took him away to jail. He was given no reason for his arrest.

A few hours after von Braun's arrest, General Dornberger was told to report to a conference at the office of General of the Infantry, Buhle. When he arrived, he was told that von Braun, as well as two Peenemünde engineers, had been arrested "for sabotage of the *A-4* project" and was in prison. Astounded and disbelieving, Dornberger asked for the specific charges against the engineers. Buhle was unable to tell him. Seething with anger, Dornberger charged into the offices of Field-Marshal Keitel the next morning and demanded to hear the details. When he heard the actual charges, he was amazed.

"Do you know that your colleagues have stated in

company at Zinnowitz that it had never been their intention to make a weapon of war out of the rocket? That they had worked, under pressure from yourself, at the whole business of development only in order to obtain money for their experiments and the confirmation of their theories? That their object all along has been space travel?"[34]

Dornberger didn't know whether to laugh or to cry. Von Braun had never been able to control his enthusiasm for space travel. Dornberger had repeatedly warned him about discussing it with Nazi officials, but in private most of the engineers had been willing to wax enthusiastic about the subject; even Dornberger himself had been known to discuss the nonmilitary applications of the rockets. The objective of their research was military, but to arrest someone because they had spoken of nonmilitary uses for rockets? That was absurd! It would have been funny, except that Keitel informed Dornberger that von Braun and the other two engineers stood a good chance of being executed for their "crimes." The authorities believed that von Braun had intended to sabotage the rockets—an odd conclusion, considering his devotion to rocketry—and escape to the West in a small plane, taking the plans for the rockets with him to England or the United States. And, in fact, von Braun did own a small plane. He flew it on weekends, usually to visit his parents or other relatives.

Dornberger learned later that the accusations against von Braun had originated with a young female dentist whom he had met at a cocktail party. He had spoken freely with her about his theories of space travel—too freely, as it turned out—without realizing that she was an agent of the *Gestapo*.

The *Gestapo*! So that was it! This was Himmler's way of striking back at von Braun for refusing to work for him!

Angrily, Dornberger made the rounds of the Nazi authorities, repeatedly stating his confidence in von Braun and the others and urging that they be released. Though he tried to speak with Himmler himself, the *Gestapo* chief refused to give him an audience.

According to Albert Speer's memoirs, it was his intervention that finally saved von Braun from being tried and possibly hanged as a traitor. "When Hitler visited me at my sickbed in Klessheim," Speer wrote, "and treated me with such surprising benevolence, I took this occasion to intercede for the arrested specialists [von Braun and the other engineers], and had Hitler promise that he would get them released. But a week was to pass before this was done and as much as six weeks later Hitler was still grumbling about the trouble he had gone to. As he phrased it, von Braun was to be 'protected from all prosecution as long as he is indispensable, difficult though the general consequences arising from the situation' were."[35]

After two weeks in jail von Braun was released, having never been informed of the reasons for his imprisonment. Dornberger met him at the jailhouse door, with a large bottle of brandy.

But Himmler may have had the last laugh after all. As Speer put it, "Himmler had achieved one of his ends. From now on even the top men of the rocket staff no longer felt safe from his arbitrary hand. It was conceivable, after all, that I might not always be in a position to free them if they were arrested again."[36]

However, when the rocket engineers were next threatened by the complicated political machine of the Third Reich, the threat came not from the *Gestapo* but from Hitler's bullying private army, the SS. And this time it wouldn't be Albert Speer who saved them but Wernher von Braun's quick thinking.

And the U.S. Army.

5 "The rocket worked fine. It just hit the wrong planet."

The building of the *V-2* rockets continued through 1943 and into 1944. Even as the rockets were being manufactured in large quantities, the rocket engineers continued to test rockets at Peenemünde, sending design changes to the Mittelwerk factory every few days as improvements were made.

At Blizna, in southern Poland, a training ground was set up where soldiers could be taught to fire *V-2*s. It was at this site, one day in 1944, that von Braun was nearly killed. Von Braun later described the incident:

> It chanced that one day I was standing in an open field looking at a time indicator at the top of a tower which announced that a rocket was just about to arrive in the target area. Imagine my horror when I glanced up in the direction from which it was expected, to see a thin contrail moving toward me! There was barely time to fall flat on the ground before I was hurled high into the air by a thunderous explosion, to land unhurt in a neighboring ditch. The impact had taken place a scant 300 feet [90 m] away and it was a miracle that the exploding warhead did not grind me to powder.[37]

Dornberger, who was standing nearby, also came close to being pulverized by the rocket. Apparently, neither man had been aware that tests were still proceeding, late in the afternoon.

An interesting scheme had been developed for actually firing the *V-2*s. Hitler and the engineers alike had wanted to build reinforced bunkers, permanent installations from which rockets could be fired westward toward England and other countries. But Dornberger had protested and eventually won the day. It was Dornberger's idea that the rockets should be fired from movable platforms so that a *V-2* firing site could be set up overnight, the rockets fired over the course of a few hours, then the platform moved to a new site with fresh rockets. This way, the Allies would be unable to pinpoint a single *V-2* firing installation and bomb it, as they had Peenemünde.

As it turned out, Dornberger's scheme was more appropriate than even he had suspected. By the time the *V-2*s were fully operational, Hitler's armies were in heavy retreat from the Allied forces. It was desirable to move the *V-2* firing platforms as close to enemy lines as was prudently possible, but by late 1944 the enemy lines were changing daily, drawing inexorably inward toward Berlin, the capital of Hitler's Third Reich. Even as the first mobile *V-2* launching pads were trundled toward their launching site, Hitler's dream of European conquest was crumbling around them.

September 7, 1944: the first pair of operational *V-2*s were fired in warfare. The target wasn't London, the city with which the rocket was to become identified, but Paris. One rocket fizzled out and fell short, but the other one struck at the Porte d'Italie, causing minor damage.

The next volley of *V-2*s, fired on September 8 from just outside the Hague, Netherlands, struck London. Three people were killed. Here is an excerpt from a report on the incident by British Air Chief Marshal Sir Robert Hill, published in the *London Gazette* after the war:

At approximately 20 minutes to 7 on the 8th September [1944] Londoners on their way home from work or preparing for their evening meal were startled by a sharp report which sounded almost, but not quite, like a peal of thunder. At 1843 hours (6:43 P.M.) a rocket fell at Chiswick, killing 3 people and seriously injuring another 10. Sixteen seconds later another one fell near Epping, demolishing some wooden huts but doing no other damage.[38]

This was only the beginning of a concentrated offensive in which twenty-six of the *V-2* rockets were launched against London in ten days. Then the bombing ceased. Days passed before Paul Goebbels, Hitler's minister of propaganda, announced publicly that the *V-2* rockets were the secret German weapon that had been rumored for some time. The bombing of London was then resumed, for seven months. The last *V-2* fell on London on March 27, 1945. During that period, 1,027 *V-2* rockets were launched. Seventy-nine of them failed, and the rest were fired at a number of targets in western and northern Europe, though London was the most heavily bombarded. Each rocket carried more than 2,000 pounds [900 kg] of explosives as payload.

During this period, according to the Hill report, "518 [rockets] had fallen within the London Civil Defence Region. . . . Altogether 2,511 people had been killed and 5,869 seriously injured in London, and 213 killed and 598 seriously injured elsewhere. These figures would have been substantially smaller but for a number of unlucky incidents, in which rockets chanced to hit crowded buildings."[39]

How did von Braun feel about the devastation wrought by the rockets he had helped to build? Publicly, he supported the war effort, if rather unenthusiastically. But to a reporter after the war, he said, "The Allies had bombed us several times at Peenemünde, but we felt a genuine regret that our missile, born of idealism, like the airplane, had joined in the business of killing.

a London street after a *V-2* attack in 1945

We had designed it to blaze the trail to other planets, not to destroy our own."[40]

At the time of the first *V-2* firing on London, when asked by a friend how the rocket had performed, von Braun put it more succinctly: "The rocket worked fine," he said. "It just hit the wrong planet."

Not all of the engineers shared von Braun's feelings on the matter. Erick Bergaust quotes another, unnamed Peenemünde engineer as having told him, some years after the war: "Don't kid yourself. Although von Braun might have had space dust in his eyes since childhood, most of us were pretty sore about the heavy Allied bombing of Germany—the loss of German civilians, mothers, fathers, or relatives. When the first *V-2* hit London, we had champagne. Why not? Let's be honest about it. We were at war, and although we weren't Nazis, we still had a Fatherland to fight for."[41]

Even as the *V-2* was being developed, manufactured, and fired, von Braun's mind was turning toward even more powerful rockets, rockets that could be used to launch satellites into orbit around the earth, rockets that could carry human beings into space. Only one of these rockets ever got beyond the drawing-board stage, and that just barely, but some of them represented significant leaps in the technology of rocket flight.

The planned *A-6, A-7,* and *A-8* rockets were little more than variations on the *A-5* and *A-4* (*V-2*); they were never built. The *A-9* was something else again. It would have been launched like a rocket, but it would have glided to a landing on airplanelike wings.

Does this concept seem familiar? It should. The *A-9* was the precursor of the present-day space shuttle. Since von Braun worked briefly on the space shuttle project toward the end of his life, it is likely that the *A-9* is the true linear ancestor of NASA's reusable spacecraft. Unlike the space shuttle, however, the *A-9* would never have gone into orbit around the earth. Instead, it would have carried materials and passengers over a range of roughly 400 miles [640 km] in about seventeen minutes.

The *A-9* rocket, however, was only part of a grander scheme in von Braun's mind. He wanted to make it part of a two-stage rocket. The idea of staging a rocket had been developed by Tsiolkovsky; it involved placing one rocket on top of one or more other rockets. As each *booster* or *stage* exhausted its fuel, it would be dropped away, and the one above it would be fired. In this man-

ner, the rocket would have sufficient tank space for large
amounts of heavy fuel, yet each tank could be dropped
away when it was no longer needed, allowing the rocket
to become lighter, and therefore faster, as it rose. The
rocket that von Braun envisioned as the first stage (that
is, the rocket underneath) of the *A-9* was the *A-10*. This
rocket would have had a thrust of 200 tons. It would
have boosted the *A-9* to a height of 40 miles (64 km),
then floated back to earth on a parachute as the *A-9*
leaped into outer space. As a weapon of war, the *A-9/
A-10* could have dropped bombs on New York City
from a launching site in Germany. As a peaceful spacecraft, it could have orbited satellites around the earth
and carried human beings into space.

An *A-11* rocket was envisioned but never fully designed. It would have been a monstrous rocket with the
capability to carry humans to the moon, as large as the
Saturn 5 rocket that von Braun would build years later
for this purpose.

The *A-9* was actually built, under the name *A-4B*. It
was launched twice, the last time at the beginning of
1945. The first time it rose about 100 feet (30 m), then
crashed into the sea. The second time it rose 50 miles
(80 km), traveling at almost 3,000 miles (4,800 km) per
hour. It was the most advanced rocket that the Peenemünde team built, but research was cut short by the
end of the war.

By January 1945, the war was indeed grinding to an
end. Hitler was losing. Supplies were dwindling, and
German troops were overwhelmed by the superior num-
bers of their enemy. The Allied armies were now encroaching on Germany itself, and Berlin, where Hitler
kept his main headquarters, would soon fall.

Wernher von Braun knew that within months, perhaps even weeks, Peenemünde would be overrun by
Allied troops, quite possibly Russians. The Allies would
be interested in capturing as many rocket parts, and as

many rocket engineers, as they could get their hands on.

There would also be forces within the dying Third Reich that would try to see to it that this did not happen. During 1944, the rocket engineers had come under the supervision of the SS, Hitler's elite army. General Dornberger had been eased out and replaced by SS General Kammler, a ruthless, efficient, and brutal soldier. Von Braun knew that when the Allied troops arrived, Kammler might kill the rocket scientists rather than allow them to fall into the hands of the enemy. Or he might take them captive, using them as hostages or bargaining chips to secure his own freedom.

What should the rocket scientists do? The Nazi hierarchy had a few ideas of its own, but in the confusion at the end of the war many of those ideas were contradictory. As von Braun put it later, "I had ten orders on my desk. Five promised death by firing squad if we moved, and five said I'd be shot if we didn't move."[42]

In effect, von Braun had been given a free ticket. Since all possible actions—including no action at all—had been forbidden him, he was free to do as he chose. The consequences would be equally dire either way. In mid-January 1945, he held a meeting of the top scientists at Peenemünde and talked the problem out. Rumor had it that the Russians were approaching Peenemünde from the south and would be arriving soon. If the engineers simply remained at Peenemünde, they might be killed in battle or taken hostage by the SS. Otherwise, they would certainly be captured by the Russian troops and taken to the Soviet Union, along with case after case of captured rocket parts. Was this what the scientists wanted?

No, they decided, quite unanimously. None of them wanted to live under the Russians. Neither did they want to be captured by the British or the French, both of whom had fought against Germany in the war. Unanimously, the group decided that they must surrender to the Americans before they fell into the hands of the Russians. If nothing else, the Americans were the most likely to give them a free hand in rocket research after the war. Or, as one of the scientists explained it later, rather undiplomatically: "We despise the French; we are mortally afraid of the Soviets; we do not believe the British can afford us, so that leaves the Americans."[43]

This meant that they had to get away from Peenemünde, go into hiding until they had the opportunity to surrender to American troops. And somehow they had to smuggle all of their papers and important equipment out of Peenemünde, because they certainly would be expected to resume their rocket research once they were in the United States. And they couldn't allow more than a decade's worth of work to be lost, either to the Soviets or to the ashes of war.

Before the engineers could leave Peenemünde, von Braun received a bizarre order from the army commander in charge of the local defense. Von Braun and his engineers were to become soldiers and fight the Russians when they arrived at Peenemünde. The idea appalled him. As the Third Reich collapsed, there was no chance that Peenemünde could be saved. At best, the engineers would find themselves Russian prisoners, the very fate they had hoped to avoid.

But another set of orders arrived at the same time, from General Kammler. The SS general ordered von Braun to move the engineers from Peenemünde to Thuringia, near the Mittelwerk factory. There, they would be safe from Russian capture.

Von Braun considered the two alternatives. The scientists would certainly be captured if they stayed at Peenemünde, but Kammler's plan was probably the first step in a plan to turn the scientists into SS hostages. The SS general wanted them all in one place, where he could keep an eye on them. When the time came, they would become the pawns in his negotiations with the Allies.

Neither alternative looked very desirable, but by following Kammler's orders they would at least have a chance to evacuate Peenemünde. Once in Thuringia, they could play it by ear. Von Braun announced to his fellow engineers that they would be heading south.

With the help of a rather mysterious assistant named Erich Nimwegen, who had a knack for procuring materials and equipment through barely legal methods, von Braun prepared to evacuate thousands of individuals, including engineers, technicians, workmen, and their families, from Peenemünde to Thuringia. It was a massive operation. But von Braun insisted that the evacuation must proceed in an orderly fashion: "We will go as an organization," he told the others. "This is important. We will carry our administration and structure straight across Germany. This will not be a rout."[44]

The evacuation of Peenemünde was perhaps the greatest test yet of von Braun's leadership ability. At Peenemünde he had showed that he could organize teams of engineers to perform technical miracles through hard work and careful planning, and that he could persuade politicians, such as Hitler, of the importance of his work. But now he was caught up in a nation crumbling under the pressures of losing a war; his organization was perhaps only days away from being captured by Russians; and they may well have been flinging themselves into the arms of an even worse menace. Yet the organization held together. Von Braun's evacuation did not degenerate into chaos.

In addition to evacuating people, it was necessary to move large quantities of papers and materials. Von Braun's assistant, Dieter Huzel, later recalled the immensity of the job:

We went to work with a vengeance. Virtually all the coordination came through von Braun's staff, and this kept us busy night and day. Such simple things as the procurement of boxes for packing was in itself a large task. Some of the technical sections needed hundreds of them. We devised a color-coding system for ready identification of each box on arrival at our new head-quarters: white for administration, green for design and development, blue for manufacturing, red for test, and so forth. All this time each department was frantically trying to determine which thirty percent of their people were not to be taken along, and how many of the seventy percent who were going had families, and how many people were in these families.[45]

Finally, a convoy was organized, in which the thou-sands of engineers, workers, and other Peenemündians would be transported to their new destination via train, truck, car, and any other method available. For the first load, more than five hundred personnel were loaded onto a freight train, where they slept in beds of straw in freight cars. Cows were also sent along in the freight cars to provide milk for the babies of the fleeing parents.

Von Braun knew that there were dangers present in moving the Peenemündians away from Peenemünde. At least one authority had ordered them to stay at Pee-nemünde and fight; hence, if caught they could be ar-rested for desertion and summarily executed. But von Braun's assistant, Nimwegen, solved this problem with a brilliant stroke.

Shortly before the evacuation, Peenemünde had been given a batch of stationery with a new letterhead, iden-tifying them as a branch of the SS rather than the army. But the printer had badly mangled the letterhead. It was supposed to read BZBV Heer, the name of an organization within the SS. Instead, the printer had printed the name as VABV, the initials of a nonexistent organization.

With a flourish, Nimwegen invented a top-secret
agency with the initials VABV, the full name of which
translated into English as Project for Special Disposi-
tions. This meant nothing but sounded impressive. With
this secret organization behind him, von Braun could
claim to be acting under the orders of Himmler himself,
and no one would dare to question him.[46]

The name VABV was painted on boxes and arm-
bands, trucks and cars—anything that might be in-
spected by SS agents or other authorities encountered
on the road south. The trucks and cars were then packed
full of equipment and prepared for a convoy to the
south.

Before the trip began, von Braun climbed on board
his small airplane and flew to the nearby farm of his
relatives the Von Quistorps, whom he had visited frequently during the previous years. The Von Quistorps
were already preparing to move to a safer area near
Holland. While visiting, von Braun spoke briefly with
his sixteen-year-old cousin Maria, whom he had known
for years. Although von Braun did not speak of it with
her, his feelings for her were becoming more than just
those of a fond cousin. He was falling in love with her.

Then he returned to Peenemünde and began the series of convoys that carried the equipment from the test
site to its new residence to the south. The cars and
trucks were stopped frequently by SS agents, but the
VABV ruse worked. The equipment got through without question.

On February 27, 1945, von Braun took his last look
at Peenemünde. That night, as the automobile in which
he was riding hurtled through the mountains in the darkness, both von Braun and the driver fell asleep. Von
Braun awoke to find himself tumbling helplessly down
a cliffside. When it crashed at the bottom the driver
was killed, and von Braun suffered a broken arm and

fractured shoulder. He lapsed into unconsciousness and woke to find himself in a hospital bed.

He was in bad shape, but there was no time for a slow recovery. His arm was set hastily in a splint, and in a short time he was back supervising the transfer of equipment. Eventually, the Peenemünde staff and the equipment that they had ferried were gathered in an area called Bleicherode.

As spring approached, events proceeded at a hasty clip. In early March the Russians captured Peenemünde. Less than three weeks later, the Americans captured the Mittelwerk factory. Nervous about the encroaching armies, Kammler ordered that the top rocket scientists, including von Braun, be moved to the village of Oberammergau, site of the famous religious ceremony known as the Passion Play, performed there every ten years.

Von Braun and five hundred of his engineers were separated from their families and taken to Oberammergau by train. On arrival, they were placed in a small internment camp. "The scenery was magnificent," von Braun said later. "The quarters were plush. There was only one hitch—our camp was surrounded by barbed wire."[47]

It was obvious that Kammler was holding them there as hostages, as von Braun had feared. As long as they were all in Oberammergau together, where Kammler could keep his finger on them, their fates were in the hands of the SS. Somehow, they had to get out of Oberammergau, but that was easier said than done. They were guarded constantly by the SS.

On a sudden inspiration, von Braun pointed out to the head SS guard that the Oberammergau area could easily be bombed by one of the Allied airplanes that frequently passed overhead. One bombing run could eliminate all of the major rocket scientists of the Third

Reich. Any SS officer who allowed such a thing to happen would surely be court-martialed.

The guard agreed but said that there was no way to transport the scientists out of Oberammergau. Von Braun, who had already considered this possibility, told the guard that he could get some cars, if necessary. In fact, von Braun had already arranged for twenty cars to be brought to Oberammergau by drivers formerly employed at Peenemünde. The guard allowed the scientists to move to other villages in the Oberammergau area, reducing the risk that they would all be killed in a single airstrike. One of the scientists then convinced the SS guard that he would be safer in the event that they were captured by Americans if he removed his SS uniform and put on civilian clothes. The frightened officer agreed. From that point on, all SS surveillance of the scientists ceased.

They had won their freedom; now the scientists had to carry out their plan of surrendering to the American army before Kammler could bargain their lives away to the highest bidder. But where *were* the Americans?

"Unfortunately for us," von Braun said later, "the American army was a long way off. General Patton's tanks apparently had less gas than we."[48]

Desperate for food and supplies, the scientists put the VABV signs back on their cars and requisitioned materials from local army supply posts. Then von Braun, who was still suffering from the results of his car crash, checked into a hospital, where his arm was rebroken and set again. For three days he lay in a hospital bed, listening to Allied bombs exploding all around the building. Finally, a soldier appeared at von Braun's bedside, escorted him to a waiting ambulance, and drove him to see his old friend and commanding officer, General Dornberger.

Dornberger had set up a retreat in a resort hotel, Haus Ingeborg, in the town of Oberjoch, along with two dozen of the Peenemünde engineers. Von Braun's brother Magnus was there.

There wasn't much to do at Oberjoch except play card games and wait for the Americans to arrive so that they could surrender to them. On May 1, they heard on the radio that Berlin had fallen and Hitler was dead. In fact, Hitler had committed suicide rather than be taken prisoner by the Allies, but the Germans would learn this only belatedly.

Surprisingly, the war was not yet over; Germany continued to fight. But the scientists decided that the time had come nonetheless to surrender to the Americans. The advancing troops were drawing near, and the scientists could simply go to meet them. But a large group of Germans might appear hostile to the Americans; a single volunteer was needed to approach the troops. Wernher's brother Magnus was chosen, because he had a speaking knowledge of English.

On the morning of May 2, 1945, Magnus pedaled off on a small bicycle, to meet the advancing Americans. It was the beginning of a new phase in the life of von Braun and the others, a phase that would culminate in the launching of a manned rocket to the moon.

6 "Did you ever try to kill Hitler?"

The first American Magnus encountered was the sentry for the Antitank Company of the 324th Infantry Regiment, 44th Infantry Division. The company was stationed in the German village of Schattwald, on the Austrian border. The young American sentry, Private First Class Frederick P. Schneikert, did not know at first what to make of the young German on the bicycle.

"Komm vorwarts mit die Hande hoch!" he shouted, pointing his rifle meaningfully in Magnus's direction.

Magnus, who had been prepared to speak with the Americans in English, was startled to find an American speaking with him in German; later, he would learn that Schneikert had picked up a smattering of German from his grandmother in Sheboygan, Wisconsin. However, he had no trouble divining the American's meaning: "Come forward with your hands up!" He climbed down from his bicycle and raised his hands. In a polyglot of German and English, Magnus explained his mission to the American private.

Schneikert was baffled and not at all sure what to do. Like most American soldiers at the time, he was distrustful of Germans, soldiers and civilians alike. This young man who claimed to be a rocket scientist was doubly suspicious, so he turned the matter over to his commanding officer, First Lieutenant Charles L. Stewart.

Stewart was also suspicious of Germans, and with good reason. Only two days earlier he had come within seconds of being killed in *two* booby traps rigged to catch unsuspecting troops and was still nervous about these close calls with death. Warily, he began to interrogate the young von Braun.

At first, the interrogation was a comedy of errors. Magnus patiently, if semicoherently, explained that his brother was Wernher von Braun, Germany's top rocket scientist, and that he wished to surrender to the Americans. Stewart, not entirely able to follow the German's polyglot English, mistakenly believed that Magnus was trying to *sell* his brother to the Americans, a betrayal that Stewart found personally offensive. However, the misunderstanding was soon cleared up. Stewart gave Magnus passes for the scientists and guaranteed their safe passage to the American encampment.

Magnus returned to Haus Ingeborg, at Oberjoch, and explained what had happened. Several of the scientists, including Wernher von Braun and Dornberger, piled into three BMW automobiles and drove to the American camp.

The Americans were immediately struck by Wernher von Braun. He was young, handsome, charming—and his arm jutted out in front of him in a thick white cast. He did not cut the figure one might expect of Germany's chief rocket scientist. Nonetheless, the Americans understood that they had a prize here. Now, they had to figure out what to do with it.

By the next day, reporters and photographers were arriving to interview von Braun and take his picture. These first reporters were from army newspapers and public relations offices, but it would not be long before von Braun found himself a focus of attention for civilian reporters as well. Fortunately, von Braun had always loved this kind of attention, at least from the days when he had stood in front of the department store in downtown Berlin explaining the workings of Oberth's *Kegeldeuse* to passersby. And he knew the value of publicity. With good spirits, von Braun posed for photograph after photograph in his stiff white cast, smiling broadly for his audience.

Once in American custody, von Braun and the scientists from the Oberjoch retreat were moved to a detention camp at Garmisch-Partenkirchen, where they found themselves reunited with many other engineers and scientists with whom they had worked at Peenemünde. As the Americans tried to figure out what to do with these captured scientists, von Braun and the others found themselves with a considerable amount of time on their hands. They spent it, in part, writing up lengthy descriptions of the work that they had performed at Peenemünde. Magnus von Braun even organized an amateur theater company and produced a musical version of Oscar Wilde's *The Importance of Being Earnest*, for which he wrote the lyrics and played the starring role.

As the American military became increasingly aware of the rocket scientists, the scientists were subjected to an increasing number of questions, many of them naive and laughable: "Did you ever try to kill Hitler?" "Did you ever try to kill Roosevelt?"[49] The scientists answered the questions as best they could and waited until the Americans made up their minds about what they were going to do with them.

At this point, U.S. Colonel Holger N. Toftoy entered the picture . . . and Operation Paperclip began.

Toftoy was one of the first military officers to reach the Mittelwerk factory after it was captured by American troops. His mission was to ship a hundred *V-2* rockets back to the United States, where they could be analyzed and tested. This was easier said than done. It had been the practice of the Germans to wait until the very last minute to assemble a *V-2*, to guarantee that

Wernher and his brother Magnus flash happy smiles after surrendering
to American troops on May 3, 1945.

the rocket would be fresh and fully tested when it was fired. What Toftoy found at Mittelwerk was an assortment of disparate parts, with no indication of which parts were actually used in a *V-2* or how to put them together into a finished rocket. Worse, the area containing the Mittelwerk factory was in the Soviet zone, the portion of Germany that was to be turned over to Russian troops for occupation. Toftoy had barely more than a month to get the *V-2* parts out before the Russians arrived and claimed them for their own. And, unknown to Toftoy, the Americans had agreed to give the British *at least* half of the rocket equipment that they uncovered, further complicating his task.

Because Toftoy was unaware of the agreement with the British, he proceeded as though it did not exist, shipping *V-2* parts back to the United States as rapidly as his resources would allow. In the United States, the *V-2* parts were shipped to the White Sands Proving Grounds in New Mexico.

But what to do with the parts once they arrived? No one had thought to include an instruction booklet with this *V-2* jigsaw puzzle—"Attach wing A to hull B"—and even the brightest rocket scientists in the United States were literally decades behind the scientists who had built the rockets. Who was going to tell them how to put the rockets together?

When Toftoy heard that the top rocket scientists had surrendered and were being held by the 44th Infantry, he had the answer. He recommended to the army that the German scientists be brought to the United States—which, of course, is what von Braun's group had intended all along. The German scientists could then show the army how to put the rockets together, how to fly them, and perhaps even how to build better ones.

Toftoy was made chief of the Rocket Division in the Office of Research and Development Service of the Office of Chief of Ordnance—a mouthful of a title that meant he was to create a guided-missile program for the United States. This put him in a position to tell Washington that he needed three hundred German scientists to help him do the job.

When he met von Braun and the others, he found that they were quite amenable to the idea, but Washington was somewhat less so. The Germans had very recently been our enemies, these scientists had built rockets that had taken the lives of innocent civilians in England and elsewhere, and there were those in the U.S. government who wanted them kept out of the country, perhaps even punished as war criminals. (As it turned out, at least one of the rocket scientists *was* a war criminal, though this information was not made public until the late 1970s, as we'll soon see.)

But on July 19, 1945, the U.S. Army Joint Chiefs of Staff authorized Operation Overcast, described in a secret memorandum as a "project of exploiting German civilian scientists, and its establishment under the Chief, Military Intelligence Service. . . ."[50] Shortly thereafter, however, the project was renamed Operation Paperclip, in reference to the ubiquitous metal clips used to identify the dossiers of relevant scientists.

Negotiations proceeded apace between the German scientists and the United States, with Toftoy caught in the middle. The Germans wanted a three-year contract; the United States would allow only six months. The Germans wanted to take their families with them; the United States insisted that the families remain in Europe, at least until the eventual disposition of the scientists, beyond the initial contract, was determined. When the Germans balked at leaving their families, the United States promised to build a camp for their dependents, where they could be guaranteed an acceptable quality of life. Part of the scientists' pay would be channeled to their families.

And how much would the Germans be paid? Von

Braun's salary was the highest—$750 a month, a very respectable income for the mid-1940s. Others received less, down to the technicians, who would receive $162 a month.

The final sticking point was the number of German scientists that would be allowed to come to the United States. The U.S. government insisted that Toftoy bring no more than a hundred, but he could not bring himself to prune the number down that low. In spite of his orders, he brought 115.

Operation Paperclip came in for serious criticism at the time from those who objected to the importation of Germans—many of whom were former members of the Nazi party—into the United States, where they were placed on the payroll of the American government. And, in recent years, it has become apparent that the army team behind Operation Paperclip played fast and loose with some of the background facts concerning the German scientists. At least one of the rocket scientists brought into the United States under Paperclip—Arthur Rudolph, who built rocket engines at Peenemünde and later became an important figure in the American space program—had committed war crimes in Germany. The Paperclip officials, however, chose to ignore this fact and to alter records that might have led to Rudolph's prosecution. Eventually, in the late 1970s, Rudolph was identified as a war criminal and was deported. He had been one of those responsible for the heinous treatment of concentration camp victims at Mittelwerk.

However, the records of several other scientists, including von Braun himself, were also altered to make them more acceptable. In most cases these alterations were minor, and only occurred after the scientists had been in this country for two years, but they are worth noting.

In the 1980s, journalist Linda Hunt obtained several

of the Paperclip documents through the Freedom of Information Act and demonstrated, in an article for *The Bulletin of the Atomic Scientists* and in a television documentary, how those documents had been altered. For instance, here is the initial wording of a security evaluation written about von Braun in 1947, when von Braun was being considered for U.S. citizenship:

Based on available records, subject is not a war criminal. He was an SS officer [during the period when Peenemünde was under SS control] but no information is available to indicate that he was an ardent Nazi. Subject is regarded as a potential security threat by the Military Governor, Office of Military Government for the U.S. A complete background investigation could not be obtained because subject was evacuated from the Russian Zone of Germany.

Except for the part about von Braun being a "potential security threat," this is not a particularly damning report, but it did threaten von Braun's ability to gain U.S. citizenship and remain in the United States as a working scientist. The report was surreptitiously altered to read:

Further investigation of subject is not feasible due to the fact that his former place of residence is in the Russian Zone where U.S. investigations are not possible. No derogatory information is available on the subject individual except NSDAP records, which indicate that he was a member of the [Nazi] Party from 1 May 1937 and was also a Major in the SS, which appears to have been an honorary commission. The extent of his Party participation cannot be determined in this Theater. Like the majority of members, he may have been a mere opportunist. Subject has been in the United States more than two years and if, within this period, his conduct has been exemplary and he has committed no acts adverse to the interest of the United States, it is the opinion of the Military Governor . . . that he may not constitute a security threat to the United States.[51]

As it developed, von Braun proved not only to not "constitute a security threat to the United States," but to instead constitute a considerable asset. Still, the manner in which his records were doctored was illegal and is a shameful episode in government operations. In von Braun's case the results were benign, but in the case of Arthur Rudolph, who worked with von Braun and was a genuine war criminal, a serious miscarriage of justice was perpetrated.

If you read closely, you'll note that the reports mention that von Braun was a member of the Nazi Party. Considering von Braun's general dislike of the Nazis and the party apparatus, this comes as something of a surprise. In fact, as the report indicates, he joined in 1937. Thirty years later, he explained to a British reporter why he had joined:

> When I first began my studies in 1932, I wasn't forced to enter the Party, but I did have to take part in these student exercises if I wanted to remain a student. I became a Party member when I was an assistant professor in Berlin, which meant being an employee of the government. There was no choice. Suddenly there would be a letter in the mail which said, "We are extremely happy that you are elected to become a member of the Party because of your good behavior. Heil Hitler, and your Party payments are due next March." If one hadn't joined one would have lost one's job. Employment is a means of doing the work you want to do and to forgo all this would be a hard decision. Many people who joined the Party had the philosophy that you retained your own thinking even if you were a member. In that way you might even be in a position to do more good.[52]

Wernher von Braun arrived in the United States in September 1945. His port of entry was Boston, Massachusetts, but he remained there only long enough to catch a boat to Fort Strong, on Long Island. At the fort, which at that time was run by the Army Intelligence Service, von Braun and six other former German rocket scientists sat for two weeks, being interrogated and playing all-night games of "Monopoly."

Most of the scientists were then shipped to the Aberdeen Proving Grounds in Aberdeen, Maryland, where they were reunited with 14 tons of notes and records that they had compiled at Kummersdorf and Peenemünde. Their job was to sort and classify these papers, a formidable task. Von Braun, however, was shipped to a different destination: Fort Bliss, Texas.

He made the trip by train, in the company of Major James Hamill. Hamill's job was to see to it that von Braun had minimal contact with other people on the train. The war was only recently over and dislike of Germans was still strong; von Braun's safety could be endangered if his fellow passengers found out that he was a former Nazi.

As the train approached the Texarkana station, however, the gregarious von Braun fell into conversation with a traveling American businessman. The rocket scientist found it difficult to guide the discussion away from personal details.

The businessman asked von Braun where he was from.

Thinking quickly, the rocket scientist said that he was from Switzerland, which would explain his thick accent.

The businessman, however, turned out to be intimately familiar with Switzerland, from his many trips there. Delighted to discover that von Braun was Swiss, he asked the rocket scientist what line of work he was in.

"Steel," replied von Braun, still improvising.

The businessman was thrilled. He was in the steel business, too. He was anxious to swap notes with von Braun about their common experiences with the Swiss steel market.

Just as von Braun was running out of ways to avoid

the subject, the train arrived at Texarkana. The businessman rose to leave, then turned to shake von Braun's hand. "If it wasn't for the help you Swiss gave us," he proclaimed, "there's no telling who would have won the war!"[53]

Finally, the train arrived at El Paso, and von Braun was taken to Fort Bliss. In December, he was joined there by other members of his rocket team. By February 1946, the major portion of the Peenemünde engineering team had been reassembled in El Paso, and they began working with rockets again.

But von Braun was disappointed. He had imagined that a nation as rich as the United States would pour even more funds than Germany into the development of rockets. He was wrong. For one thing, it was no longer wartime. The impetus for building rockets in Germany had come not from a desire to explore space but from a desire to build missiles. The same was true in the United States. And in a time of peace, no one needed missiles. Later, missile development in the United States would be spurred on by a desire for ICBMs capable of lofting nuclear warheads across the ocean, but in the mid-1940s the U.S. government assumed that its large fleet of B-52 bombers would be adequate for this task. Hence, the money von Braun had expected for designing new rockets was not forthcoming.

Instead, von Braun was expected to launch the *V-2*s that he had built while in Germany. In the mid-1940s, in fact, the major part of the U.S. rocket program consisted of testing German-built rockets!

7

"Shooting a V-2 is a . . . dangerous business."

The testing of the *V-2*s took place at the White Sands Proving Grounds in New Mexico, not far from Fort Bliss, in Texas. (Ironically, White Sands was also not far from the New Mexico site where Dr. Robert Goddard, the American rocket pioneer, had performed his own poorly funded rocket experiments.) In 1945, three hundred freight cars filled with *V-2* parts—the same *V-2* parts that Colonel Toftoy had spirited out of the Mittelwerk factory after the war—had arrived at White Sands. It was the job of von Braun and the other German scientists to put these parts together to make *V-2*s—and to put those *V-2*s through a wide variety of tests.

The *V-2*s were not the first rockets tested at White Sands. During World War II, the army had tested a pair of much smaller rockets there, called the *Private* and the *WAC Corporal*. (According to rocket historian Willy Ley, the acronym WAC stands for "without altitude control."[54]) These rockets were used for purely scientific purposes; they were not missiles. The *WAC Corporal* could carry a payload of 25 pounds (11.25 kg) to an altitude of 19 miles (30.9 km)—small potatoes by *V-2* standards—and had been used for atmospheric tests.

With the acquisition of the *V-2*s, American rocketry took a quantum leap forward, albeit with borrowed German technology. But a certain breaking-in period was required before the testing could be considered successful. By 1946, the *V-2* equipment was already growing old and the American expertise in rocket launching—even with German help—was still minimal.

The Germans taught the Americans how to launch *V-2*s. "That job took eight months," von Braun said later. "We seemed to be expected to do it in two weeks, but shooting a *V-2* is a complicated and dangerous business. Especially the rusty, dried-out *V-2*s we had at White Sands. And the facilities there were unsuitable for efficient shoots."[55]

Nonetheless, the first *V-2* was launched from White Sands on April 16, 1946. For the first nineteen seconds of the flight all went well, then the rocket veered off course; one of the wings had sheared off. Fortunately, the rocket had been equipped with an emergency cut-off mechanism; the flow of fuel was turned off from the ground, by radio, and the rocket fell harmlessly into the desert. The next few *V-2* tests proceeded well, however, and not until the seventh launching did one of the rockets actually blow up.

One hundred *V-2*s had been assembled from the parts shipped to the United States by Toftoy. This meant that there would be a lot of testing. And while von Braun was active in the testing, there was little to be done in the way of original rocket design; thus, he found himself with a lot of time on his hands. In 1946, he decided that he was tired of spending that time alone. He wanted to get married. And the person he wanted to marry was his cousin Maria.

the launch of a *V-2* rocket at White Sands, New Mexico, in 1946

This, however, was rather a sticky situation. He had never discussed the possibility of marriage with his cousin; he didn't even know if she *wanted* to be married to him. And, with Maria thousands of miles away in Germany, it was difficult to broach the subject casually. Unsure of what to do, he wrote a letter to his father, the Baron von Braun, suggesting that he might want to sound Maria out on the subject—casually, of course. Perhaps the elder von Braun could ask her if she had any boyfriends, any romantic plans, whether she ever thought about her cousin Wernher in the faraway United States.

According to one account, his father decided instead to take the bull by the horns. The next time he saw his niece Maria, he put the question to her quite bluntly: "He wants to marry you! How about it? How do you feel? Will you marry him?"

"Why, I never considered anyone else," Maria replied.[56]

The baron informed his son of Maria's reply and Wernher proposed formally to his cousin in a subsequent letter. It was agreed that they would be married as soon as possible.

Complications remained, however. The course of true love may never run smooth, but in this case it had to run the gauntlet of government red tape. Wernher had to file a request to travel to Germany and marry his cousin. The request was finally processed in early 1947, and von Braun was given permission to return to Europe. However, it was also required that he be accompanied by government agents at all times. While in Europe, von Braun also arranged to accompany his parents back to America, where they would live for several years. As a result, von Braun's honeymoon party consisted not only of himself and his new bride, but also his father and mother and a team of government agents.

Back in the United States, the von Brauns settled down to a more or less normal family life. So did many of the other German scientists, whose families were finally allowed to join them, two years after Operation Paperclip had brought them to the United States.

The Germans at Fort Bliss formed a tightly knit group, dining together, taking trips across the Mexican border together, gathering in mutual support groups. But they also made an attempt to adapt as thoroughly as possible to their adopted country, to become American. They spoke in English whenever possible. They were quite aware that many American engineers resented their presence in the American rocketry community, as though in some manner they were superior to the Americans. If they wanted to be assimilated into America, they knew they would have to play a careful game of office politics at Fort Bliss.

In 1947, the Germans and their families were given the opportunity to apply for U.S. citizenship. However, a loophole in the immigration laws soon reared its head. Because they had been brought into the country as part of a secret government operation, they had never *officially* entered the country and could not become citizens. The solution? The scientists left the country briefly and came back in, making their arrival official. Several of them, including von Braun, chose to go to nearby Juarez, Mexico. While there, they stopped at the American consulate and filled out the requisite forms for an American visa. Then they entered the United States on the Juarez trolley. The method of entry was stamped officially on their citizenship applications, along with the cost of the trip—4¢.

Even after his marriage, von Braun found himself with time on his hands. So he turned to writing. The book that he wrote was called *The Mars Project.*

The Mars Project is sometimes termed a science fiction novel, but it isn't, really. It has no characters and not much of a plot. It is filled with abstruse mathematics and is almost unreadable by the technically unenlightened reader.

The Mars Project is actually a work of thoughtful speculation on the future of the Space Age, describing in considerable detail the way in which von Braun believed the first expedition to Mars would take place.

The mission to Mars was one of von Braun's lifelong dreams. The idea excited him much more even than the idea of going to the moon. It would be a much greater feat, technologically, much more difficult to achieve. The trip itself would take much longer—months or even years to reach Mars as compared to a few days to reach the moon.

Most of all, von Braun wanted to scotch the myth that a trip to Mars could be accomplished, as it had been in a number of science fiction stories, by a handful of adventurers who build a spaceship in their backyard and pilot it to the moon like a flying Winnebago. In *The Mars Project*, seventy astronauts travel to Mars in ten spaceships, as part of an expensive government-sponsored project, not unlike the later Project Apollo.

Though the book was brilliantly thought out, von Braun had a hard time selling it to a publisher. Looking at it today, it isn't hard to understand why. It is by no means light reading. Here is a typical passage from the book:

Neglecting the finite length of the power track, it was found that in the orbit of departure the velocity change of $v'_1 = 3.31*10^5$ cm/sec^{-1} would be required (equation (21.4)) so that the ship might have a residual velocity of $v_{d,1} = 3.03*10^5$ cm/sec^{-1} when leaving the earth's gravitational field. At the perihelion of the home voyage, the ship will now overhaul the earth from "astern" and enter tellurian gravity, having the same velocity difference $v_{d,4} = v_{v,1}$.[57]

Not the sort of book you'd like to curl up with on the beach, unless you have a summer job calculating spacecraft trajectories.

Von Braun finally sold the book to the University of Illinois Free Press, but only after his name had become sufficiently well known to guarantee a certain minimum of sales. It was published in 1953.

V-2 testing at White Sands proceeded throughout the late 1940s. *V-2*s were used to determine the best trajectories for rocket launchings, the maximum distance the small rocket could travel, and the maximum altitude to which it could soar. The rockets were equipped with sensitive equipment to monitor conditions in the upper atmosphere. In one memorable series of tests a *V-2* became the lower stage of a two-stage rocket, the upper stage of which was the small *WAC Corporal*. The resulting combination was dubbed a "Bumper" *WAC*, because the *V-2* could "bump" the small rocket to a much higher altitude than either of the rockets could achieve on its own.

On February 24, 1949, a Bumper *WAC* rocket achieved an altitude of 250 miles (400 km) above the New Mexico desert. It was the highest that any rocket had ever flown at that time and represented pretty much the culmination of what could be done with *V-2* rockets. If more significant steps in rocketry were to be made, bigger and more advanced rockets would need to be built.

However, as fate would have it, the next step in the Space Age would not take place at White Sands. Perhaps it is significant that the last tests of the Bumper *WAC* combination were performed, in 1950, not at White Sands but at a new site in Florida called Cape Canaveral.

8

"She is eight minutes late. Interesting."

In 1950, the German rocket scientists were moved *en masse* from Fort Bliss in Texas to the army's Redstone Arsenal in Huntsville, Alabama. In one sweeping gesture, Huntsville was transformed from the home of a moderately important army base to the rocket-manufacturing capital of the United States. And the Germans, who had originally come to this country on six months' probation, found themselves transformed into Americans.

It's not hard to imagine the culture shock inherent in a community of German immigrants, many of them recently members of the Nazi Party, moving into a medium-sized, all-American, southern community within five years of World War II. Certainly the citizens of Huntsville had little idea of what to expect, and the Germans probably had scarcely more of an idea what to expect from Huntsville.

The Germans knew that Huntsville was to be a more permanent home than El Paso, which had been merely a waystation on the road to other things; they might remain in Huntsville for the rest of their lives. And so, upon arriving in Huntsville, they plunged deeply into the life of the city, determined to become as all-American as anyone who had been born there. Their children were entered into public schools, they joined

Von Braun with his wife, parents, and daughter Iris in Huntsville, Alabama.
He later had a son, whom he named Peter.

community organizations, and they made as many
friends as possible among the native Huntsvillians.

Before long, the barriers of suspicion that existed
initially between the citizens of Huntsville and the Germans broke down. The rocket scientists found themselves accepted as American citizens, which most of
them became, officially, within two years of their arrival
in Huntsville. Of course, it didn't hurt that the rocket
engineers brought a needed infusion of money to the
Huntsville economy.

Von Braun was named head of the U.S. Army's
Guided Missile Division of the Rocket Research Center
at the Huntsville Arsenal. With his wife, parents, and
his daughter Iris (who had been born in El Paso in

1948), von Braun settled down in Huntsville to a life as a U.S. citizen. (His parents moved back to Germany in 1953, when his father received a pension from the German government that he was not allowed to collect while living in the United States.)

During his years at Huntsville, von Braun's literary career—which had begun with *The Mars Project* a few years earlier—blossomed. For instance, he wrote a series of articles for *Colliers* magazine, discussing future directions for the space program. Several articles discussed the possibility of landing human beings on the moon and Mars, others the importance of placing a space station in orbit around the earth as a stepping stone to further exploration. In 1953 von Braun published a book titled *Across the Space Frontier*, in collaboration with several other experts on space exploration, which covered many of the same topics that von Braun discussed in the *Colliers* articles. Von Braun even served as technical adviser on several Walt Disney feature documentaries about spaceflight. (It seems likely that von Braun was one of the inspirations behind the Disney cartoon character Professor Ludwig von Drake, a German-accented duck scientist who made his debut around 1960.)

With each publication and new movie, von Braun's reputation grew. He became known as a charismatic public figure, a man who could communicate his enthusiasm for space travel to the general public. Many people who had never previously considered the possibility of exploration beyond the earth's surface were introduced to this idea through von Braun's articles, books, and the Disney films with which he was involved.

With his new title, von Braun had become a man of considerable importance in the army missile program, but the next great leap in his career came when he was assigned to build a new rocket, one that would be the next step beyond the *V-2*. This rocket was to be called the *Redstone*, in honor of the arsenal at which the German engineers worked.

The *Redstone* was twice as large as the *V-2*, standing 70 feet (21 m) tall, and it had a thrust of 78,000 pounds (35,100 kg); the maximum thrust of the *V-2* had been 55,000 pounds (24,750 kg). Since the weight of a fully fueled *Redstone* was 60,000 pounds (27,000 kg), it had room to spare for a payload of about 8,000 pounds (3,600 kg), which it could carry over a horizontal distance of some 200 miles (320 km). By lightening the payload somewhat, it might even have been possible to loft it high enough to send it flying into outer space . . .

This line of thought gave von Braun an idea. The *Redstone* was intended as a medium-range guided missile, but it might just be capable of launching a small satellite into orbit around the earth.

The idea of an artificial earth satellite had been in von Braun's mind since he was a boy. It had been discussed by both Tsiolkovsky and Oberth and was considered a necessary first step on the road to conquering space. In fact, the basic idea behind the satellite predated even the idea of space travel; it had originated in the mind of the brilliant scientist Isaac Newton in seventeenth-century England.

Basically, the idea of an artificial satellite is this: If you fired a cannon from the top of a high mountain—the method suggested, perhaps not altogether seriously, by Newton himself—the cannonball would fall back to earth on a long curving path, carried horizontally by its momentum and downward by the earth's gravity. Since the earth is round, a cannonball fired with sufficient velocity would fall past the curve of the earth itself and continue falling forever, chasing the ground as a dog chases its tail. It would become an *artificial* satellite of the earth in the same way that the moon, falling around our planet in exactly this manner, is a *natural* satellite of the earth.

Of course, no cannon exists with the power to put a cannonball in orbit about the earth. And a cannonball fired from the top of a mountain would soon be slowed by air friction and fall back to the ground—if it didn't run into another mountain first.

But with a rocket as powerful as the *Redstone* in place of a cannon, and a tightly sealed package of instruments in place of the cannonball, it might be possible to loft the satellite above the earth's atmosphere, where it could coast freely through space.

Von Braun believed that he now had the capability to launch such an artificial satellite around the earth. The satellite could contain instrumentation for carrying out important experiments that could only be performed in space. And it would demonstrate the possibility that human beings could be launched around the earth, and eventually to other planets, in larger capsules, boosted by more powerful rockets, which von Braun was convinced that he could build.

Excited by this idea, von Braun wrote up a formal proposal that he called Project Orbiter, which he submitted to the U.S. government in 1954. In this proposal, he suggested that he be allowed to use a modified *Redstone* rocket to launch an earth satellite. He could do so, he said, within two years—by 1956. Because Project Orbiter would be put together almost entirely out of existing, thoroughly proven technology, it was nearly guaranteed to be successful. And it would give the United States a tremendous boost in international prestige to become the first country to launch a satellite into outer space.

Von Braun foresaw that the United States might eventually have competition in this endeavor from other countries, such as the Soviet Union, so it would be necessary to move quickly if this country were to maintain a technological edge. What he may not have foreseen is that he himself would have competition in this endeavor from within the U.S. armed services, and that this competition would kill his chances for being the first to launch a satellite—and hand that opportunity to another country altogether.

Right about the time the Project Orbiter proposal was submitted, an international committee decided that an eighteen-month period in 1957 and 1958 would be designated the International Geophysical Year—IGY, for short—a period during which scientists would expend a great deal of effort to learn as much as possible about the planet earth. As part of this "year," the United States had made a commitment to launch an artificial satellite. The Soviet Union had made a similar promise, though many people doubted that they had the technological expertise to do it.

The White House took von Braun's Project Orbiter, sponsored by the U.S. Army, under advisement as a possible satellite for the IGY. But a second satellite proposal was submitted at about the same time by the U.S. Navy. This proposal was called Project Vanguard.

When the time came for a decision to be made as to which project would receive funding, the White House put its weight behind the navy project. Vanguard became the U.S. satellite program. Von Braun was told to go back to building missiles.

Not surprisingly, von Braun was furious. He was the nation's leading expert on rocketry and he knew it. He had a working rocket that would be capable of launching a satellite. The navy, on the other hand, had only a proposal. The equipment that would launch the *Vanguard* satellite hadn't even been built yet. Von Braun knew that he could launch a reliable satellite *years* ahead of the navy. And yet the White House would not allow him to. And by denying him the chance to launch a satellite, they were running the risk that the Soviet Union would launch one first.

Why was von Braun's orbiter proposal turned down? There were several reasons. The most important was that it was perceived as being a military project, one that would use military hardware—a rocket conceived as a missile and a descendant of the German *V-2*—to put a satellite into orbit. The *Vanguard* satellite, on the other hand, would be launched by a rocket designed purely for scientific research. Dwight D. Eisenhower, the president of the United States, was vehemently opposed to the militarization of the American space program. As a former military man—in fact, as one of the greatest military figures of this century—he understood as well as anyone the danger of maintaining a hostile military stance during peacetime, and he feared that the rest of the world would misinterpret the significance of a satellite launched by a missile. They would see it not as a scientific endeavor but as a none-too-subtle demonstration of America's prowess at building missiles.

In addition, the legal status of satellites had not yet been determined. An American satellite, orbiting the earth every ninety minutes or so, would pass over a large number of foreign countries, including the Soviet Union. In international law, a nation's airspace could be considered as extending indefinitely into the sky above that nation, or at least as high as the orbit of the moon. A satellite might be considered a hostile encroachment on a nation's borders; wars had been fought over less. It would seem only prudent to divest a satellite of all possible military significance before subjecting it to this ultimate test of international law.

Another possible reason for the decision to go with the navy proposal rather than the army proposal was a general prejudice against the German-run army missile program. To some people, it might not have seemed fitting that America's first satellite be launched by a group of people who were seen by some as "second-class citizens." Some historians have cited this as a compelling reason behind the decision in favor of Project Vanguard.

But there is yet another reason that is less often discussed. The Eisenhower White House simply wasn't interested in being first into outer space. It was of little importance to administration officials that the Soviet Union might well launch the first artificial satellite into orbit around the earth. They believed it would be perceived by the world at large as a minor scientific achievement. They felt the Russians were entitled to an occasional scientific triumph, as long as it didn't hurt American prestige. And the White House was convinced that a failure to be first into space would not hurt American prestige.

As it turned out, they were quite wrong.

It is hard to guess what went through von Braun's mind as he seethed with anger over the rejection of Project Orbiter. But some historians have suggested that he may have planned a sly rebellion against the powers-that-be in the U.S. government. For one brief moment in 1956, von Braun may have come very close to launching an unauthorized satellite into orbit around the earth. If he had done so, the history of the Space Age might have been quite different. But the White House was apparently wise to the trick that von Braun may or may not have been about to play and put a stop to it at the last minute.

On September 21, 1956, von Braun assembled on the launching pad the largest American rocket up until that time. It was a *Jupiter-C*, a modified version of the *Redstone* consisting of four stages, each a rocket in its own right. Like the Bumper *WAC*, each stage would "bump" the ones above it to a higher altitude, so that the entire configuration would be capable of reaching great heights. In fact, the *Jupiter-C* was so powerful

111

that the top stage would have gone directly into orbit— if it had been fueled.

And, in fact, this may have been von Braun's intention. With a live top stage, von Braun could have launched a satellite that day—the first artificial earth satellite in history. It would have been a simple matter. Perhaps that is what he planned to do.

But someone in the White House noticed what was going on. The order came down only hours before launch: Put sand in the top stage, not fuel.

By this time, von Braun was working for the newly organized Army Ballistic Missile Agency (ABMA), under the direct command of Major General John B. Medaris. Word came down to Medaris from Lieutenant General James M. Gavin in the Pentagon: "I'm holding you personally responsible to see that there are no accidents."[58]

"Accidents," of course, did not refer to exploding rockets but to accidental satellites. Medaris's career was on the line. He leaned on von Braun. The top stage was filled with sand. By its own choice, the United States did not launch a satellite in 1956.

The *Jupiter-C* test was nonetheless spectacularly successful. The rockets fired precisely on schedule. They soared 700 miles (1,120 km) upward and 3,300 miles (5,280 km) horizontally, a record distance.

More *Jupiter* launchings followed this, but von Braun was still restrained from launching a satellite. Further, owing to competition between the various armed services in the development of missiles, it began to be rumored that von Braun might lose all authority to build long-range missiles, which were considered the province of the air force. The navy was to build intermediate-

the launch of a *Jupiter-C* rocket

range missiles, which would be fired from ships. This left little rocket research for the army, and therefore for von Braun.

For a time, it began to look as though von Braun would never realize his dream of space travel, at least not while working for the army, an organization to which he felt he owed a certain allegiance. But events on the far side of the globe were already in progress that would propel the United States kicking and screaming into the Space Age.

When the Soviets arrived at Peenemünde at the end of World War II, they found a few rocket scientists and a smattering of *V-2* parts. Both the rocket scientists and the *V-2* parts were taken back to the Soviet Union, where they were wrung dry of all information they contained. Then they were discarded, and the Soviets built their own space program on the foundation of knowledge they had thus acquired.

The key figure in the Soviet space program was Sergei Pavlovich Korolev. He was to the Soviets what von Braun was to the United States, a man with the knowledge of rockets and the drive to turn that knowledge into reality.

During World War II Korolev built jets in a prison camp in Siberia, a captive of his own government. But after the war he was put to work building missiles.

In the mid-1940s, the Soviets were very interested in missiles. This was primarily because they were in the process of developing an atomic bomb, a weapon that the United States had developed in the waning days of the war. The atomic bomb was useless without a method of dropping it on the enemy. The United States had used bombers for this purpose—at Hiroshima and at Nagasaki, the only times that the bomb had been used in the war—but the Soviets lacked a bomber fleet as impressive as the one the Americans had. Instead, they chose to build rockets, very large ones, to carry atomic bombs (and later the more powerful hydrogen bombs) in the event of nuclear war.

Soviet politics are volatile; shifts of leadership are not common, but when they happen they are abrupt. The leader who initiated this spate of missile building was Josef Stalin, but Stalin chose to keep the missile capability secret. When Stalin died in the early 1950s and Nikita Khrushchev rose to power, the new Russian leader was startled to find that the Soviets possessed a battery of powerful rockets.

Khrushchev wanted desperately to show Russian missiles to the world, to let other nations know that the Soviet Union was as capable as—perhaps more capable than—the United States was of waging nuclear war.

But who would believe him? The world saw the Soviets as technologically backward. He would be laughed at if he claimed otherwise. It would be necessary instead to demonstrate the Soviet skill at making rockets.

But how? He could hardly launch a missile at another country to prove it could be done. He wanted to impress the rest of the world, and perhaps frighten the United States, but he didn't want to start a war.

Sergei Korolev offered Khrushchev the answer to his dilemma. Like von Braun, Korolev wanted to launch a satellite. And, like von Braun, Korolev knew that the missiles he had built for carrying bombs would be perfect for conquering space.

But where the Eisenhower Administration had no interest in the propaganda value of a satellite, Khrushchev was interested in precisely that. In 1957, he gave Korolev permission to launch an artificial satellite into orbit around the earth.

On October 4, 1957, Korolev did so. The satellite was called *Sputnik*, a name that translated very roughly as "traveler of the earth."

It stunned the world.

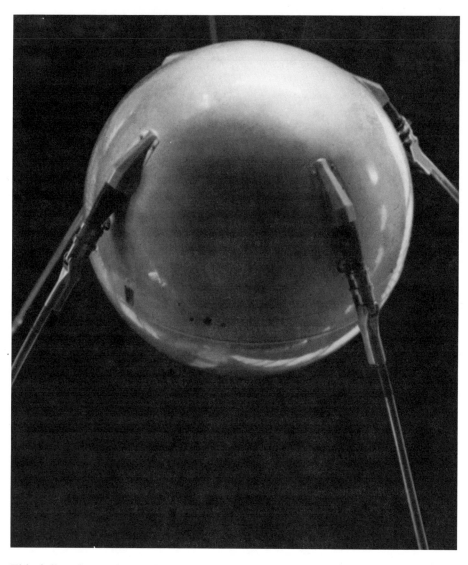

This full-scale mock-up of *Sputnik 1* was put on display at the Paris Air Show in France in 1961.

Von Braun heard about *Sputnik* while at a dinner with the secretary of the army and the head of the joint chiefs of staff. In his book *Countdown to Decision*, Medaris described how von Braun "began to talk as though he had been vaccinated with a phonograph needle."[59]

"We knew they were going to do it," von Braun shouted. "*Vanguard* will never make it. We have the hardware. We can put up a satellite in sixty days."

Medaris interrupted: "No, Wernher. Make it ninety days."[60]

The world at large did not miss the point of *Sputnik*. The Soviet Union gained immensely in respect as their satellite swung in tight circles around the earth. And the smug assurance many Americans felt toward their country's technological superiority suddenly disappeared.

Congress demanded an investigation to find out why the United States had not launched a satellite first. Had the Soviets gotten better German rocket scientists than America had? (They hadn't, but for a time it was rumored that they had.)

Foreign newspapers questioned the technological capabilities of the United States. International polls showed that respect for the Soviet Union had (appropriately enough) skyrocketed, while respect for the United States was diminished.

And, still, the Eisenhower Administration was baffled by the reaction. *Sputnik* was just a hunk of metal, a "silly bauble in the sky," as one presidential adviser phrased it.[61]

Von Braun was nonetheless given permission to prepare for a satellite launching. *Vanguard*, however, would be given the first chance to win back America's lost honor.

Alas, Project Vanguard was not ready to launch a satellite. The project had been underfunded and understaffed almost since its inception. Nonetheless, the navy team prepared a rocket, and on December 6, 1957, an attempt was made to launch it.

It rose a few feet from the launching pad. Then it fell back and exploded.

It was a spectacular failure. The film of the explosion became a classic depiction of Space Age disaster, occasionally popping up on television even today, often to humorous effect.

Headlines around the world—and even in the United States—ridiculed the failure. The American satellite was nicknamed "Flopnik" and "Kaputnik."

By January 29, 1958, von Braun had prepared his own launch vehicle, another variation on the *Redstone* called the *Juno*. (This game of changing rocket names was designed, at least in part, to obscure the fact that the launch vehicles had originally been designed as missiles.) The rocket, and the tiny satellite perched atop it, sat on the launching pad at Cape Canaveral, Florida, waiting for the launch signal. But high-velocity winds in the upper atmosphere canceled the flight. The next day, January 30, conditions had not changed, and the flight was canceled again.

The next day the winds were still high, but they looked as though they were about to slack off. A decision was made to launch anyway. At the last moment the winds did indeed slack off. Conditions were perfect for launching a satellite.

At 10:47:56 P.M. EST, January 31, 1958, the launch signal was transmitted. The rocket rose from the launch pad in a cloud of smoke. Within seconds, it was lifting into the sky. Within minutes, it had disappeared.

But had the satellite gone into orbit?

Von Braun was not at the Cape. He was far away, at the Pentagon, just outside Washington, D.C.

When word came that the launch was successful, von Braun announced to the small group of spectators

The artificial satellite *Explorer 1* is launched into space aboard a *Jupiter-C* rocket on January 31, 1958, marking the United States' first entry in the space race.

around him that the satellite would pass over California in exactly 106 minutes. At that time—precisely 12:41 A.M. EST—a listening station in San Diego would pick up a signal from the satellite, and they would know that it had gone into orbit.

With all eyes focused intently on the clock, von Braun and his companions waited for the word from California.

At 12:41, Dr. William Pickering of the Jet Propulsion Laboratory, who was waiting with von Braun, put in a call to San Diego. Had they heard the satellite?

No, they replied.

Two minutes later he asked again. Had they heard the satellite?

No.

Where was it, they wondered. Had something gone wrong?

"Why the hell don't you hear anything?" Pickering yelled into the phone.

The others in the room turned to von Braun and asked him for an explanation. Could the satellite have failed?

Suddenly Pickering looked up from the phone. "They hear her, Wernher, they hear her!"

Von Braun looked at his watch and said calmly, "She is eight minutes late. Interesting."[62]

9 "...one small step for a man..."

The satellite that von Braun launched was called *Explorer 1*. By the time of its launching the Soviets had placed a second *Sputnik* in orbit. This one carried a live dog on board. Facetious headline writers called it "Muttnik."

Sputnik 1, the first Soviet satellite, weighed 184 pounds (83 kg). *Sputnik 2*, the second Soviet satellite, weighed a whopping 1,121 pounds (504 kg). How much did *Explorer 1* weigh? Ten-and-one-half pounds (4.7 kg). Soviet premier Khrushchev called it a "grapefruit."

The truth was, the Russian rockets were more powerful than the American rockets. They had greater thrust and could lift much larger satellites into orbit.

The late 1950s and early 1960s were a time of great tension and competition between the United States and the Soviet Union. Historians call this period the "Cold War." With the launching of the first satellites, the competition between these two superpowerful nations moved into outer space. The race to put bigger and better satellites into orbit was soon dubbed the "space race."

Although the Soviet satellites were bigger, the American satellites were not without merit. The original *Sputnik*, for instance, contained no instruments other than a radio transmitter that broadcast a continuous stream

Four of the scientists who played key roles in the launching of the *Explorer 1* are shown at a press conference following the event. *From left to right:* Dr. William H. Pickering, Dr. Edward Manring, Dr. James Van Allen, and von Braun.

of beeps back to earth. But *Explorer 1* contained a radiation detector that discovered intense rings of radiation encircling the earth at a great altitude. These rings of radiation became known as the *Van Allen radiation belts*, after James Van Allen, the scientist who designed the experiment.

Sputnik showed that rockets could be used to launch satellites into orbit around the earth. Von Braun's *Explorer* showed that satellites could perform important scientific work.

But, to the world at large, the space race wasn't about science. It was about missiles. By launching larger satellites than the United States, the Soviet Union was demonstrating that it could launch larger missiles, and therefore larger bombs. And this hurt U.S. prestige around the world in a way that no "mere" scientific achievement could repair.

Sputnik was a major propaganda victory for the Soviets. To counteract the effect of this victory, and restore wounded American pride, it would be necessary for the United States to perform some spectacular feat in space before the Soviets did. This would tell the world that the United States took second place to no other nation—especially not the Soviet Union—in its ability to wage technological warfare.

And what more spectacular feat could the United States perform than putting a human being into orbit around the earth?

Ironically, the failure of the United States to launch a satellite into orbit around the earth before the Soviets probably furthered Wernher von Braun's dream of space travel more than any successful U.S. rocket launching could have.

If it had not been for the space race—the intense competition between the United States and the Soviet Union—the U.S. government, in the late 1950s, would never have considered putting a human being in orbit around the earth. But the space race changed everything.

In 1958, Wernher von Braun and his team of army rocket engineers submitted a follow-up proposal to Project Mercury. It was called Project Adam, and its goal was to place a man into space. (The idea of female astronauts was still several years in the future.) It was taken very seriously by the government. At the same time, a civilian organization called the National Advisory Commission for Aeronautics (NACA) produced a similar proposal for a project to put men into orbit around the earth.

The Eisenhower Administration still had little interest in space exploration, but the pressure from the public and from Congress was intense. Reluctantly, Eisenhower dissolved NACA in 1958, re-formed it as a brand-new agency called the National Aeronautics and Space Administration (NASA), and charged it with the job of putting a man in space. This, at least, put the space program in civilian hands and took it away from the military, as the Eisenhower Administration had desired all along.

The venture to put a man in space soon became known as Project Mercury, after the swiftest of the Roman gods. Von Braun very much wanted to work on a project to put a man in space, but as an army employee he was unable to participate in the civilian Project Mercury. NASA, however, was interested in having von Braun involved in the program. A bitter power struggle ensued between NASA and the army over who would get the services of von Braun and his team of rocketeers. NASA won. In 1960, the rocket team left the Army Ballistic Missile Agency and formed NASA's brand-new George C. Marshall Space Flight Center—without ever leaving Huntsville.

The idea behind von Braun's proposal for Project Adam was that a *Redstone* rocket could be used to boost a small capsule containing a human passenger into a short flight through outer space. The capsule would not orbit the earth; the *Redstone* was not powerful enough to boost such a large object into orbit. Rather, it would go up and come right back down again, like an arrow that had been fired straight up into the air.

It would be a short flight—what aerospace experts call a *suborbital flight*—but it would demonstrate that humans could travel in space. And it would test possible designs for space capsules and space suits.

It would also give the United States a chance to beat the Soviets in the space race.

Project Adam was rejected by the Pentagon in 1958. But shortly thereafter most of the ideas from Project Adam became part of Project Mercury.

The goal of Project Mercury was to put a man into orbit around the earth. The seven test pilots selected to fly in Project Mercury were called *astronauts*. The rocket that would place them in orbit was the *Atlas*, which had been designed by the U.S. Air Force as a long-range missile. The *Atlas* was larger and had greater thrust than von Braun's *Redstone* rockets.

But the *Atlas* would not be ready to fly until roughly 1962. The first Mercury flights, planned for 1960 or 1961, would use *Redstone* rockets to launch astronauts into short suborbital flights, exactly as von Braun had suggested in his Project Adam proposal.

Originally, it was intended that all seven astronauts would fly suborbital flights on a *Redstone* rocket before anyone flew an orbital flight on an *Atlas*. As it turned out, only two astronauts flew suborbital flights. On May 5, 1961, astronaut Alan Shepard, Jr., took a fifteen-minute hop into space in a small capsule nicknamed *Freedom 7*. On July 21, 1961, Virgil ("Gus") Grissom made a similar flight in the capsule *Liberty Bell 7*. (The "7" in the capsule names referred to the seven Mercury astronauts.) Shepard's flight went flawlessly. Grissom's was marred only at the end when his capsule, floating in the Atlantic Ocean while Grissom waited to be picked up by helicopter, filled with water and sank.

These were the last suborbital flights in Project Mercury. Even as they were taking place, an emergency decision was made to begin orbital flights with the third mission.

What was the emergency? On April 12, 1961, even

The Project Mercury astronauts, who comprised the first U.S. astronaut team. Front row, from left to right: Walter M. Schirra, Jr., Donald K. Slayton, John H. Glenn, Jr., and Scott Carpenter; back row: Alan B. Shepard, Jr., Virgil I. "Gus" Grissom, and L. Gordon Cooper.

before Alan Shepard flew his suborbital mission, a Soviet cosmonaut (the Soviet equivalent of an astronaut) named Yuri Gagarin became the first person in outer space. And Gagarin's mission was no mere suborbital flight. He actually orbited around the earth once.

The United States had lost another round in the space race. Once again, Americans found themselves following on the heels of the Soviets.

On February 20, 1962, astronaut John Glenn (who later became a U.S. senator from Ohio) became the first American, and the third human being, to orbit the earth. (The Soviets, in the meantime, had launched a second cosmonaut, Gherman Titov, who orbited the earth for a full day.)

Glenn was proclaimed a national hero and his flight was an occasion for tremendous excitement. Yet an air of anticlimax hung over it. The Soviets, after all, had done it first.

Several months earlier, the newly elected American president, John F. Kennedy, had grappled with the problem of gaining a propaganda victory over the Soviets in the space race. What could the United States do to impress the world that offered a better-than-fair chance of success against the Soviets?

After questioning a battery of experts, including von Braun and his own vice-president, Lyndon Johnson, who had been a major force behind much space-age legislation, Kennedy had his answer. On May 25, 1961, less than three weeks after Alan Shepard's suborbital flight and a month and a half after the orbital flight of Yuri Gagarin, Kennedy went before Congress and announced that, before the decade of the 1960s was over, the United States would place an astronaut on the moon and bring him safely back to earth.

Despite his interest in placing a human being in space, Wernher von Braun was not heavily involved in Project

Von Braun instructs President John Kennedy and Vice-President Lyndon Johnson, both strong supporters of the space program, on plans for new rockets being built at the Redstone Arsenal in Huntsville, Alabama.

Mercury. Even as his *Redstone* rockets were boosting astronauts into suborbital flight, von Braun was involved in a much more advanced project. He was building the largest rocket yet constructed in the United States, a rocket that would rival the giant boosters used in the Soviet Union and that could carry entire crews of astronauts into orbit around the earth. Von Braun named this rocket the *Saturn*, which was the next planet in the solar system after Jupiter; hence, the *Saturn* would be the next major rocket to follow von Braun's *Jupiter* series. If it were successful, it would lead to an even larger rocket, a rocket that could send a spaceship to the moon.

128

Work on the *Saturn* had begun while von Braun was still working for the army. When von Braun moved to NASA, the *Saturn* project moved with him.

The *Saturn 1* was designed between 1958 and 1959. It would be a multistage rocket with a clustered engine—that is, the first stage would be made out of multiple rocket engines, bound together in a single "skirt," like a package of hot dogs. The clustered engines would be fired simultaneously, effectively combining the thrust of several smaller rockets into one large rocket.

The first *Saturn 1* rocket was tested on October 27, 1961. The rocket was 150 feet tall (45 m) and 21 feet (6.3 m) thick at its base. The test of the rocket went flawlessly. In fact, all ten tests of the *Saturn 1* rockets went off flawlessly, or at least as flawlessly as any rocket tests before or since. It was perhaps the only time in von Braun's career that he found himself with a rocket that did not need to have the bugs worked out of it.

Even as the *Saturn 1* was being built and tested, NASA was well into planning for the moon mission. The moon program was given the name Project Apollo. Between Project Mercury and Project Apollo, astronauts and engineers alike would prepare for the moon voyage through a series of two-man missions in a program called Project Gemini.

Would the *Saturn 1* be the rocket used in Project Apollo? No. It was not powerful enough to go to the moon—a pity, since it worked so well. However, the first phase of Project Apollo would be a series of three-man orbital missions that would test the equipment to be used on the actual voyage. For these missions, a modified version of *Saturn 1* would be used, called *Saturn 1B*. This rocket would also be developed by von Braun's team.

But what of the actual moon trip? What rocket would be used for this part of the program? Obviously, it would need to be a very powerful rocket, but would it

be another variation on the *Saturn* or a brand-new rocket?

This was a subject of considerable debate around NASA and within von Braun's Huntsville team, in the late 1950s and early 1960s. What kind of rocket went to the moon would depend on the overall plan for the moon trip. Initially, two different methods for getting to the moon were contemplated. One, favored by NASA, was called *direct ascent*. The other, favored by von Braun, was called *earth-orbital rendezvous*, or *EOR*.

Direct ascent was the method that had been pictured in decades of science fiction novels and movies. The rocket would take off from the surface of the earth, turn around in space, use its powerful rockets to brake its flight, land on the moon, then take off again for earth when the mission was complete. The rocket would be like a chartered bus. It would simply go from point A to point B and back again.

But direct ascent would require an extremely large, powerful, and reliable rocket. That rocket was tentatively given the name *Nova*, and several designs for it were put on paper. If direct ascent were given the go-ahead, von Braun's team would build the *Nova* rocket. It would be the largest rocket ever built, by a considerable margin, because it would need to carry—and lift—all of the fuel necessary for leaving earth's gravity, braking against the moon's gravity, and leaving the moon's gravity.

Earth-orbital rendezvous, on the other hand, would require a pair of less powerful rockets. The first would

A *Gemini IV* spacecraft is launched from Cape Kennedy (now Cape Canaveral) in Florida on June 3, 1965. The Gemini program was carried out in preparation for the Apollo program, which would send people to the moon.

launch a large fuel tank into orbit. The second would rendezvous—that is, link up with—the fuel tank the next day and refuel, then take off for the moon. The advantage of this method was that the rocket that actually went to the moon would not carry the fuel for the entire trip. A smaller rocket, which could be refueled in earth orbit, would suffice. This was the method favored by von Braun.

Which mode did NASA choose? Neither one.

In the early 1960s, even as NASA was debating the relative merits of direct ascent and EOR, an employee of NASA named John Houbolt realized that there was a third method, which came to be called *lunar-orbital rendezvous*, or *LOR*. In this method, the lunar spacecraft would be made up of three modules, one in which the crew lived, one to carry the power supply and rockets, and one that could fly to the surface of the moon and get back to earth from lunar orbit. The spacecraft would go into orbit around the moon, two of the three astronauts would enter the third module (called the Lunar Module or, jokingly, the Bug), and fly it down to the moon. When their mission to the moon was complete, they would fly back and rejoin the main spacecraft and head back to earth.

The advantage of this method is that the entire spacecraft would not have to land on the moon. Only a small, light module would land, and it would need relatively little fuel to land and take off. A big booster rocket would only be needed to get the spacecraft off the surface of the earth. The smaller rockets in the modules would be able to handle the rest of the mission.

It was the perfect method of going to the moon. It would use less fuel than the other methods, require less brand-new technology—only the Lunar Module would need to be built from scratch—and it wouldn't require the monstrously large *Nova* rocket. A modified *Saturn* could handle the job of getting the spacecraft off of the earth. And yet, when Houbolt suggested the idea to NASA officials, they rejected it out of hand.

Their main objection was that LOR was too risky. It was felt at the time that rendezvousing—bringing together—two spacecraft in orbit was a risky business. If it had to be done, it should be done in earth orbit. If a rendezvous in earth orbit failed, the astronauts could simply be brought back to the surface, none the worse for the experience. But if a rendezvous in lunar orbit failed, the astronauts would be too far away to save. Nothing could be done. They would remain in lunar orbit until they died.

EOR used an earth-orbit rendezvous, so it was safe. LOR used a lunar-orbit rendezvous, so it wasn't safe.

Houbolt disagreed. His calculations showed that LOR was just as safe if not safer than the other methods, and it was certainly superior in all other ways. Perhaps most important of all, it almost guaranteed that the lunar mission could be put together before the end of the decade—as John F. Kennedy had promised.

Houbolt spread the gospel of LOR like a fervent evangelist. And, gradually, it began to catch on. When Wernher von Braun studied the data on LOR, he had to agree that it was indeed the best method, even though he had initially favored EOR.

In the end, LOR won out, but only after some lively debate. Von Braun later recalled an argument that ensued when he met President Kennedy's science adviser, who was bitterly opposed to LOR:

On September 11, 1962, President Kennedy visited Marshall. With the aid of a chart displayed in front of our immense first *Saturn* rocket, I explained the key maneuvers involved in LOR, when the President interrupted me and said: "I understand Dr. Wiesner doesn't agree with this." Looking into the large crowd of dignitaries, newsmen, and radio commentators in the spacious assembly building, he demanded, "Where is Jerry?" Dr. Jerome Wiesner, the President's Science

Advisor, stepped forward and said, "Yes, that's right. I think the direct mode is better." Two minutes of lively argumentation furnished exciting raw data for the media, until JFK terminated the debate and moved on. Jerry Wiesner . . . told us later that he never harbored any doubt that all three candidate modes were feasible. He just felt that with more attention to weight saving, parameter optimization and improvement of propulsion performance, even a launch vehicle of *Saturn 5* size may have sufficed for a "direct mode" flight.[63]

The *Saturn 5* was the successor to the *Saturn 1*. It would be the rocket that carried the *Apollo* spacecraft on the road to the moon. It would be the largest rocket ever built and would remain so until the Soviet Union launched the even larger *Energia* in 1987.

To launch the lunar rocket, a complex of buildings and launching pads was built on Merritt Island in Florida, adjacent to Cape Canaveral. (In 1963, shortly after the assassination of President John F. Kennedy, the complex was renamed the Kennedy Space Center. This name would later be dropped and the original name restored.) These included the so-called Vehicle Assembly Building, or VAB, the largest building in the world. The stages of the *Saturn* rocket would be put together in that building, then placed on a giant flatbed tractor that would carry it to the launching pad at a breathtaking speed of 1 mile (1.6 km) per hour.

Though most of von Braun's earlier rockets had been built in Huntsville, a special factory for the *Saturn* first stage was constructed on the Mississippi River, so that the huge rocket could be brought to the launching site by barge, the only kind of vehicle large enough to carry it over such a distance.

"You shouldn't just consider the *Saturn 5* an overgrown *V-2*," von Braun told a reporter. "That's like saying the Boeing 707 is only an overgrown Wright brothers' plane. About the only thing the *V-2* and the

Saturn 5 have in common is that they both operate on Newton's third law that every action has an equal and opposite reaction."[64]

This is perhaps an exaggeration. The *V-2* was a linear ancestor of the *Saturn 5*, if not exactly a smaller version of it, but the technological leap from one to the other was indeed large. The assembled *Apollo* craft, with the modules placed atop the *Saturn*, would be considerably larger than the Statue of Liberty . . .

John F. Kennedy had promised that the United States would land on the moon before the decade was out. By 1967, it had begun to look as if his goal would be fulfilled before that year was out, beating the deadline by a good two years.

But then tragedy struck.

The first manned *Apollo* flight was to launch a crew of three—astronauts Virgil Grissom, Ed White, and Roger Chaffee—into orbit around the earth on February 21, 1967, atop one of von Braun's *Saturn 1B* rockets.

On January 27, 1967, the astronauts entered their spacecraft, already mounted on the *Saturn* rocket, to run through a series of tests. But once they were locked inside their command module, something went wrong. A spark ignited a fire in the pure oxygen atmosphere inside the module. The astronauts yelled for help but were unable to open the hatch in time to get out. Within seconds they had been burned to death. It was the worst tragedy to strike NASA since the space program had begun and would remain the worst until the space shuttle *Challenger* explosion of 1986, nineteen years later.

It stalled Project Apollo in its tracks. The program was postponed for more than a year, while the causes of the disaster were investigated.

The problem turned out to be in the design of the *Apollo* spacecraft, not in von Braun's *Saturn* rocket.

The spacecraft was redesigned, and in 1968 Project Apollo was resumed.

But much time had been lost, and Kennedy's deadline was drawing closer. Worse, there were indications that the Soviets were preparing to make a dramatic flight around the moon, to steal America's thunder yet another time. (There was a general agreement in both the aerospace and international intelligence communities that the Soviets lacked the capability to land on the moon and take off again; their rockets weren't big enough. But a circumlunar voyage—a voyage around the moon and back—would have been spectacular enough, if they did it first.) Ironically, the Soviet space program had been slowed down in 1967 by a tragedy of its own. Cosmonaut Vladimir Koramov had died when the parachute lines on his *Soyuz 1* space capsule had become tangled and he had crashed at full velocity into the ground.

The first test of the *Saturn 5* rocket came on November 7, 1967. It was "all-up" test, which in NASA parlance meant that all of the parts of the rocket were being tested at one time, in a single launching, rather than each undergoing separate tests prior to assembly. For von Braun, this was something new. He was used to firing his rocket engines in huge test stands before he launched them into space, but there was no time for that now. If the rocket team were to put an astronaut on the moon according to schedule, the rocket had to be assembled and launched in a single test. Of course, if the test were a failure, it would be a major setback for the program.

It was not. The rocket performed flawlessly and the decision to go with the "all-up" test was vindicated, though von Braun admitted afterward that he had had serious doubts about the concept. The *Saturn 5* rose from its launch pad in a great cloud of exhaust and an explosion of sound almost as loud as a nuclear bomb.

The first manned *Apollo* flight was called *Apollo 7*; the earlier flights had been unmanned test flights. It was launched atop a *Saturn 1B* on October 11, 1968, and orbited the earth for eleven days, testing out the *Apollo* spacecraft command module.

More orbital flights had been planned before the powerful *Saturn 5* was used to send a crew of astronauts to the moon. But NASA was becoming nervous that the Soviets might steal a march on them; top officials at NASA wanted to send an *Apollo* spacecraft on a circumlunar trip, around the moon and then back to earth. Furthermore, Lyndon Johnson, who had become president when John Kennedy was assassinated in 1963, had only two months remaining in his presidency. Johnson had been one of the driving forces behind the space program since its inception, and NASA wanted to fly at least one mission to the moon while he was still in office.

The problem was, von Braun's *Saturn 5* was not quite ready. It had been given several unmanned tests and had performed well—at first. Then it was noticed that the rocket was vibrating in a peculiar manner known as "pogoing," a kind of up and down stretching motion similar to that of a pogo stick. If *Saturn 5* began to pogo during an Apollo mission, it could spell disaster for the astronauts.

But if NASA waited any longer for the *Saturn 5* to be tested again, they might lose the moon race to the Soviets. And President Johnson would not get his moon mission.

Von Braun's engineers isolated the pogo problem and cured it—or so they thought. But there was no time to test out the rocket again, because NASA had decided to send *Apollo 8* around the moon in late December.

On December 21, 1968, astronauts Frank Borman, James Lovell, and William Anders rode into the sky atop the most powerful rocket ever built. There was no

pogo effect. They were given the go-ahead to travel to the moon.

Three days later, on Christmas Eve, they went into orbit around the moon. It was a historic moment. And the Soviets had not done it first.

The next Apollo mission, *Apollo 9*, tested the lunar landing vehicle in earth orbit. *Apollo 10* also tested the vehicle, while in orbit around the moon. The lunar landing craft came within miles of landing on the moon, then returned to the Command Module.

The biggest mission of all, the one that would be given the most space in all the history books, was launched on July 16, 1969. The astronauts on board were Neil Armstrong, Edwin Aldrin, and Michael Collins. The *Apollo 11* craft went into orbit around the moon on July 19.

Later that same day, Armstrong and Aldrin piloted the Lunar Module to the moon's surface. As Armstrong became the first man to set foot on the moon—and as millions of people back on earth watched him on the world's first interplanetary TV broadcast—he uttered the words "That's one small step for a man, one giant leap for mankind." (Those who remember this broadcast, or who have seen tapes of it, might recall that Armstrong seemed to omit the word "a" in front of "man," but it was obvious what he meant to say, and this is how history remembers it.)

John Kennedy's deadline had been achieved, though only by five months. Alas, Kennedy did not live to see it.

From 240,000 miles (384,000 km) away, Wernher von

Wernher von Braun's dream is at last a reality. Video cameras demonstrate to the earthbound rocket scientists and the public at large that space travel is indeed possible, as an *Apollo 11* astronaut walks on the moon, his landing craft right behind him.

Braun watched the lunar landing on television, just like everyone else. It was the culmination of the dream that he had carried with him since he was thirteen years old.

It was also the end of the space race. The Cold War was over. The competition in space had ended on a grand note: The United States had won. The Soviets claimed that they had never actually been in the race for the moon, but few believed them.

But with the end of the space race came the end of the national impetus toward space travel. In an odd sort of way, in the moment of its greatest triumph, it was the end of von Braun's dream—and, for all intents and purposes, the end of his career.

10 "When my journey comes to an end . . ."

Like any sane human being, like anyone who loves the human race, Wernher von Braun hated war.

And yet, in one of history's bitter ironies, it was war that made his greatest triumphs possible.

It was the First World War that drove the German Army to develop new types of weapons, and thus young Wernher von Braun realized his dream of designing and building rockets. It was the Second World War and the desperation of a beleaguered nation that allowed the adult Wernher von Braun to build powerful rockets capable of flying into outer space.

When World War II ended, von Braun's resources for building rockets dried up. He found himself in the southwestern desert of the United States, showing American soldiers how to fire rockets that he had built in Germany during the war.

Then, with the advent of the Cold War between the United States and the Soviet Union, a war in which symbolic weapons played as central a role as real weapons did in a real war, von Braun once again found himself in a position to build rockets—and to send astronauts to the moon.

But by the time *Apollo 11* put its crowning touch on the space race, the Cold War was over. The competition between the United States and the Soviet Union had

141

subsided. Americans had other things on their minds. And space was not one of them.

Project Apollo was expensive. It cost billions of dollars to land astronauts on the moon. And, once the initial excitement of Neil Armstrong's first steps on the moon had subsided, a lot of people decided that there were better ways to spend that money.

Several missions remained in Project Apollo after *Apollo 11*, but the momentum of the space program was gone. Americans no longer seemed to care that much about the conquest of space.

During the years when the American space program was at its height, from roughly the time of *Explorer 1* to the time of *Apollo 11*, Wernher von Braun became probably the best-known figure in the program, next to the astronauts themselves. In fact, he was probably more famous than all but a few of the astronauts.

Despite his background as a member of the Nazi Party, as a German who had fought against America during World War II, the public liked von Braun. He was attractive. He was charismatic. He had a quick wit and a love of people. He was a family man, with three children—a second daughter, Margarit, had been born in 1952, and a son, Peter, had been born in 1960—and a wife to whom he was deeply devoted. He seemed to be deeply religious and strongly moral; these, at least, were the virtues he professed. It was easy for most people to forgive him for what he had done during the war.

For that reason, von Braun became one of the greatest popularizers of space travel. He gave lectures on the subject. He wrote books on space travel. He wrote articles for magazines, such as *Colliers* and *Science Digest*, expounding on the future of the space program. He even drew sketches of spacecraft that were turned into magnificent paintings by artists such as Chesley Bonestell.

Von Braun knew where the space program was headed, and he never hesitated to talk about it. We were going to build large space stations in orbit around the earth, he said, where astronauts could live and work for years at a time. We were going to organize a large-scale mission to the planet Mars, much like the one he had described in his book *The Mars Project.* We were going to expand outward into space just as our ancestors had expanded westward into unknown lands.

His vision of the future was a simple but dazzling one. He knew that the way to make that vision real was by discussing it with others at every opportunity, so that they would help him make it real. For a time, people really seemed to believe in his vision, and von Braun knew that it would come to pass.

And then, suddenly, the belief vanished . . .

In 1970, NASA kicked von Braun upstairs. He was quietly removed from his post as director of the George C. Marshall Space Flight Center and moved to NASA headquarters in Washington, D.C.

He was given a lavish farewell party by the citizens of Huntsville. Banners flew above the streets reading "DR. WERNHER VON BRAUN—HUNTSVILLE'S FIRST CITIZEN—ON LOAN TO WASHINGTON."

Von Braun gave an emotional speech for the occasion. "We reached high plateaus because we—the team—were standing on the shoulders of all that came before."

Waving toward the crowd, he said, "You became our most loyal supporters."[65]

Ostensibly von Braun was moving to Washington to work on plans for a manned mission to Mars. Von Braun felt that this was the next logical step in the space program. He had even written up a detailed proposal for how it would be accomplished. After all, he had been thinking about the problem for years.

Von Braun wanted to send two ships to Mars, each with a crew of six on board. The Mars craft would be spacious and roomy, at least in comparison with the Command Module of the *Apollo* spacecraft.

"We are going back to the tradition of the old sailing ships," he said. "Columbus, you will remember, took three vessels when he sailed west, and I think the record shows that he would never have returned to report his discovery had he not provided that redundancy in his system. So, if we lose one ship en route, if one ship became incapacitated and unable to return, then its six-man crew could return in the other ship. It will be a little more crowded, but it would still be entirely acceptable to return all 12 men in one ship."[66]

Von Braun believed deeply in the Mars mission, but it was not to be. President Nixon backed away from his early promises. Congress was unwilling to appropriate the money. The public had lost interest in space. And Wernher von Braun abruptly found himself with nothing to do.

For a while he worked on the early planning stages of NASA's space shuttle program, borrowing on the expertise he had gained in the design of the *A-9* and *A-10* rockets at Peenemünde, which would have flown in a space shuttle-like configuration. But soon he had contributed all he had to offer in the matter, and then there was nothing else for him to do.

Given his preeminent role in the space program, it has been suggested that von Braun should have become the director of NASA. It would have been a fitting recognition of his contribution to the American space program.

But it also would have been politically unfeasible. Von Braun's Nazi past had been forgiven but not forgotten. As a rocket scientist he was acceptable; as a top administrator, he was not.

"There was always a lingering resentment at the Washington end toward von Braun and his team," said Charles S. Sheldon, former member of the National Aeronautics and Space Council. "There were always rumors that von Braun would someday be head of NASA. But there is great sensitivity in Washington about racial and ethnic interests . . . von Braun would never be given a political position."[67]

Former NASA administrator Dr. Thomas O. Paine, referring to fellow NASA administrator James Webb (who would have been in a position to promote von Braun in the late 1960s), put it rather more bluntly: "I think Jim had the feeling that, well, the Jewish lobby would shoot him down or something. The feeling that basically you were dealing with the Nazi Party here." But Paine added,

> I think most people felt that he [von Braun] had a damned unfortunate past and nobody liked a Nazi . . . but he had kind of paid his dues and that he really helped us get to the moon in developing the *Saturn 5* and showed himself to be a worthy citizen of this country, and while we don't exactly forgive and forget, politeness dictates, at least, we won't get into a disgraceful knock down and drag out. So it was sort of a neutral thing. He was neither the terribly charismatic or popular figure Jim feared, nor was he the great target of the anti-Nazis who very properly would object to having a prominent member of the Hitler regime ensconced in Washington in a policy area.[68]

On June 10, 1972, von Braun resigned from NASA. He was sixty years old. Desiring to stay in the Washington, D.C., area, he took a job as corporate vice-president with the Fairchild Corporation, an aerospace firm involved in satellite work. Predictably, von Braun helped them to develop, and deploy, satellites.

According to those who knew him, von Braun remained healthy and vital into his sixties. In 1973, he suffered a kidney ailment and had one kidney surgically removed, but it seemed not to slow him down. He traveled frequently, indulging in a lifelong love of outdoor activities, including sailing.

Then, while visiting Alaska in 1975, he discovered one morning that he was bleeding internally. On his return to the Washington area, he checked into a hospital. There was a malignant tumor in his intestines. It was removed immediately, but apparently the disease had already spread and become inoperable. He left the hospital in September but returned in May. His health deteriorated steadily from that point on. He died on June 16, 1977, in Alexandria, Virginia.

Ernst Stuhlinger, who had been one of von Braun's fellow engineers at Peenemünde, recalled at the memorial service a statement that von Braun had made years before: "When my journey comes to an end, I hope that I can retain my clear mind and perceive not only those precious last moments of my life, but also the transition to whatever will come then. A human being is so much more than a physical body that withers and vanishes after it has been around for a number of years. It is inconceivable to me that there should not be something else for us after we have finished our earthly voyage. I hope that I can observe and learn and finally know what comes after all those beautiful things we experience during our lives on earth."[69]

How like von Braun to see death, as he saw so many things in life, as another thrilling exploration into the vast unknown that lay beyond the realm of human knowledge.

NOTES

1. Erik Bergaust, *Reaching for the Stars* (New York: Doubleday, 1960), 40.
2. Daniel Lang, *From Hiroshima to the Moon* (New York: Simon & Schuster, 1959), 182.
3. Bergaust, *Reaching for the Stars*, 43.
4. Ibid., 43.
5. Frederick I. Ordway and Mitchell R. Sharpe, *The Rocket Team* (New York: T. Y. Crowell, 1979), 13.
6. Willy Ley, *Rockets, Missiles, and Men in Space* (New York: New American Library, 1969), 153.
7. Ordway, *The Rocket Team*, 19.
8. Walter Dornberger, *V-2* (New York: Viking Press, 1954), 27.
9. Hugo Young, Bryan Silcock, and Peter Dunn, *Journey to Tranquility* (New York: Doubleday & Company, 1970), 26.
10. Lang, *From Hiroshima to the Moon*, 183.
11. Dornberger, *V-2*, 37.
12. Ibid., 23.
13. Ibid., 26.
14. Ibid.
15. Werhner von Braun, "German Rocketry (A. C. Clarke, ed.)." *The Coming of the Space Age* (New York: Meredith Press, 1966), 64–5.
16. Lang, *From Hiroshima to the Moon*, 182.
17. Ley, *Rockets, Missiles, and Men in Space*, 236.
18. Ibid., 239.
19. Dornberger, *V-2*, 64.
20. Ibid., 67.
21. Bergaust, *Reaching for the Stars*, 85–6.
22. Dornberger, *V-2*, 28.
23. Ibid., 29.
24. Ibid., 31.

25. Albert Speer. *Inside the Third Reich* (New York: Macmillan, 1972), 366.
26. Lang, *From Hiroshima to the Moon*, 184.
27. Dornberger, *V-2*, 103.
28. Bergaust, *Reaching for the Stars*, 78.
29. Dornberger, *V-2*, 157.
30. Ibid., 158–9.
31. Ordway, *The Rocket Team*, 116.
32. Bergaust, *Reaching for the Stars*, 91.
33. Von Braun, "German Rocketry," *The Coming of the Space Age*, 91.
34. Dornberger, *V-2*, 202.
35. Speer. *Inside the Third Reich*, 372.
36. Ibid., 372.
37. Bergaust, *Reaching for the Stars*, 96.
38. Sir Roderic Hill, "Air Operations by Air Defence of Great Britain and Fighter Command in Connection with the German Flying Bomb and Rocket Offensives, 1944–1945 [The Hill Report]," Supplement to the *London Gazette*, October 19, 1948. Ley, *Rockets, Missiles, and Men in Space*, 267.
39. Ibid., 269.
40. Lang, *From Hiroshima to the Moon*, 185.
41. Bergaust, *Reaching for the Stars*, 116.
42. Ordway, *The Rocket Team*, 254.
43. Ibid., 274
44. Ibid., 256.
45. Huzel, Dieter. *Peenemünde to Canaveral* (Englewood Cliffs, N.J.: Prentice-Hall, 1962), 257.
46. This version of the story is taken from Ordway's *The Rocket Team*, 257.
47. Bergaust, *Reaching for the Stars*, 110.
48. Ibid., 111.
49. Ordway, *The Rocket Team*, 274.
50. Ibid., 287.
51. Linda Hunt, "U.S. Coverup of Nazi Scientists," *The Bulletin of the Atomic Scientists*, April 1985, 41, 4.
52. Young, et al., *Journey to Tranquility*, 26–27.
53. Ordway, *The Rocket Team*, 313.
54. Ley, *Rockets, Missiles, and Men in Space*, 286.
55. Lang, *From Hiroshima to the Moon*, 188.
56. Heather M. David, *Wernher von Braun* (New York: Putnam, 1967), 112.
57. Wernher von Braun, *The Mars Project* (Urbana: The University of Illinois Free Press, 1953), 53.
58. Richard S. Lewis, *Appointment on the Moon* (New York: Ballantine, 1969), 46.

59. Kurt Medaris, *Countdown to Decision* (New York: Putnam, 1960), xxx.
60. Lewis, *Appointment on the Moon*, 53.
61. Ibid., 54.
62. Bergaust, *Reaching for the Stars*, 320–1.
63. Bergaust, *Wernher von Braun*, 408–9.
64. John Noble Wilford, *We Reach the Moon* (New York: Bantam, 1969), 135.
65. Ordway, *The Rocket Team*, 446–7.
66. Bergaust, *Wernher von Braun*, 448.
67. Ordway, *The Rocket Team*, 401.
68. Joseph Trento, *Prescription for Disaster* (New York: Crown, 1987), 89–90.
69. Ordway, *The Rocket Team*, 404.

SOURCES

Baker, David. *The History of Manned Space Flight.* Crown (New York, 1985).
——————. *The Rocket.* Crown (New York, 1978).
Bergaust, Erik. *Reaching for the Stars.* Doubleday (New York, 1960).
——————. *Wernher von Braun.* National Space Institute (Washington, DC, 1976).
Bilstein, Roger E. *Stages to Saturn: A Technological History of the Apollo/Saturn Launch Vehicles.* NASA (Washington DC, 1980).
Brooks, Courtney G., James M. Grimwood, & Lloyd S. Swenson. *Chariots for Apollo: A History of Manned Lunar Spacecraft.* NASA (Washington, DC, 1979).
Clarke, Arthur C. *The Promise of Space.* Harper & Row (New York, 1968).
——————, editor. *The Coming of the Space Age.* Meredith Press (New York, 1967).
David, Heather M. *Wernher von Braun.* Putnam (New York: 1967).
Dornberger, Walter. *V-2.* Viking Press (New York, 1954).
Goodrum, John C. *Wernher von Braun: Space Pioneer.* Strode (1969).
Hunt, Linda. "U.S. Coverup of Nazi Scientists," *Bulletin of the Atomic Scientists.* April 1985, v. 41, no. 4, pp. 16–23.
Hutton, Richard. *The Cosmic Chase.* NAL (New York, 1981).
Huzel, Dieter. *From Peenemünde to Canaveral.* Prentice Hall (Englewood Cliffs, N.J., 1962).
Lang, Daniel. *From Hiroshima to the Moon.* Simon & Schuster (New York, 1959).
Lewis, Richard S. *Appointment on the Moon.* Viking (New York, 1969).
Ley, Willy. *Rockets, Missiles, and Men in Space.* NAL (New York, 1969).

151

Longmate, Norman. *Hitler's Rockets*. Hutchinson (London, 1985).

Mansfield, Joyn M. *Man on the Moon*. Stein & Day (New York, 1969).

McDougall, Walter A. *The Heavens and the Earth: A Political History of the Space Age*. Basic Books (New York, 1985).

Medaris, John B. *Countdown for Decision*. Putnam (New York, 1960).

Nicholson, Iain. *Sputnik to Space Shuttle*. Dodd, Mead (New York, 1985).

Ordway, Frederick I., & Mitchell Sharpe. *The Rocket Team*. Crowell (New York, 1979).

Sherrill, Robert. "The Golden Years of an Ex-Nazi," *The Nation*. June 7, 1986, v. 242, no. 22, pp. 777, 792–6.

Speer, Albert. *Inside the Third Reich*. Macmillan (New York, 1972).

Trento, Joseph J. *Prescription for Disaster*. Crown (New York, 1987).

Von Braun, Wernher. *The Mars Project*. The University of Illinois Press (Urbana, IL, 1953).

―――――――――― . *Space Frontier*. Holt, Rinehart & Winston (New York, 1971).

Von Braun, Wernher, & Frederick Ordway. *History of Rocketry & Space Travel*. Crowell (New York, 1969).

Walters, Helen. *Wernher von Braun: Rocket Engineer*. Macmillan (New York, 1964).

Wells, Helen T., Susan H. Whiteley, & Carrie E. Karegeannes. *Origins of NASA Names*. NASA (Washington, DC, 1976).

Wilford, John Noble. *We Reach the Moon*. Bantam (New York, 1969).

Young, Hugo, Bryan Silcock, & Peter Dunn. *Journey to Tranquility*. Doubleday (New York, 1969).

RECOMMENDED READING

Wernher von Braun, alas, never wrote an autobiography, and the definitive biography of the rocket scientist has yet to be published. Nonetheless, a wide literature exists on the general subject of rocket development, a subject in which von Braun figures prominently, and several good histories of the *V-2* have been written. The following list includes the best books on rocketry in general, and on von Braun in particular, encountered by the author of the present work during his research and is not intended as a complete bibliography of the subject matter. A reader interested in knowing more about rocketry and space travel might start with Nicholson (1985), then move on to von Braun and Ordway (1985), Ley (1968), and Baker (1978 and 1985), though the latter is only for the ambitious. Those interested specifically in the Apollo program should read Lewis (1969), followed by Young *et al.* (1969) and Baker (1985). (Note, however, that the first two books only carry the story through the first moon landing.) For more information on von Braun and other German rocket scientists, read Bergaust (1976), David (1967), Ordway and Sharpe (1979), Ley (1968), and Dornberger (1954), though the David and Dornberger books may be hard to find. A highly fictionalized film biography of von Braun (*I Aim at the Stars*) was released in 1960 and may still appear on late-night television, but the contents should not be taken seriously.

David Baker. *The History of Manned Space Flight* (Crown, 1985) and *The Rocket* (Crown, 1978). Two exhaustive (and sometimes exhausting) histories of manned space flight and rocketry, respectively, for those readers who want to study these subjects in detail. The former contains as thorough an account of the American manned space program as you are likely to find in a single volume.

Erik Bergaust. *Reaching for the Stars* (Doubleday, 1960) and *Wernher von Braun* (National Space Institute, 1976). Two editions of the only serious adult biography of von Braun written in his lifetime. Rambling, overly chatty and far from exhaustive, but rich with anecdotes and quotes.

Arthur C. Clarke, editor. *The Coming of the Space Age* (Meredith Press, 1967). Lively collection of essays on space travel. Worth reading if only for Wernher von Braun's article on "German Rocketry," one of the few autobiographical pieces available from the rocket scientist. (Note, however, that portions of this article appear almost verbatim in the text of Erik Bergaust's 1960 book *Reaching for the Stars*, without attribution, leaving some question as to the article's authorship. Perhaps it's by von Braun "as told to" biographer Bergaust?) Also contains an excerpt from Dornberger's hard-to-find book *V-2* (see below) describing the first test of the *A-4* rocket.

Heather M. David. *Wernher von Braun* (Putnam, 1967). The best of a flood of more or less interchangeable biographies of von Braun published for young readers during Project Apollo. Hard to find, but may be in some libraries. The others are *Wernher von Braun: Rocket Engineer* by Helen B. Walters (Macmillan, 1964) and *Wernher Von Braun: Space Pioneer* by John C. Goodrum (Strode, 1969).

Walter Dornberger. *V-2* (Viking, 1954). The most entertaining and readable account of the events at Peenemünde, by one of the major participants. Quoted extensively in many later books on the subject, especially *The Rocket Team* and *Hitler's Rockets*, as well as the present volume. Out of print and hard to find but worth seeking out. A new edition is long overdue.

Richard S. Lewis. *Appointment on the Moon* (Viking, 1969). A solid historical account of the American space program through *Apollo 11*, by a reporter who was present for many of the events he writes about. An excellent introduction to the subject.

Willy Ley. *Rockets, Missiles, and Men in Space* (Viking, 1968). Classic, engagingly conversational history of rocketry by a former member of the German VfR. The material on German rocketry, from Oberth and the Raketenflugplatz through the development of the *V-2*, is especially good, if occasionally rambling.

Norman Longmate. *Hitler's Rockets* (Hutchinson, 1985). Good history of the *V-2*, with a particular emphasis on the bombing of London and the Allied response.

Iain Nicholson. *Sputnik to Space Shuttle* (Dodd, Mead, 1985). A short but reasonably thorough history of rockets and space travel, both manned and unmanned, from the 1950s to the present. Good starting point for interested readers.

Frederick I. Ordway & Mitchell Sharpe. *The Rocket Team* (Crowell, 1979). The definitive account of rocket development at Peenemünde, with additional material on the subsequent American careers of von Braun and his fellow German rocketeers. Not as entertaining as Dornberger's *V-2* but probably more objective—and certainly easier to find.

Wernher von Braun. *Space Frontier* (Holt, Rinehart & Winston, 1971). A collection of von Braun's essays on spaceflight, aimed at the reader without a technical background. Chatty and enoyable, though somewhat dated.

Wernher von Braun & Frederick Ordway. *History of Rocketry & Space Travel* (Crowell, 1969) and *Space Travel* (Harper & Row, 1985). Two editions of an authoritative history of rocketry and space travel by von Braun and rocket historian Frederick Ordway.

Hugo Young, Bryan Silcock, and Peter Dunn. *Journey to Tranquility* (Doubleday, 1969). Incisive and illuminating study of the behind-the-scenes politics that motivated Project Apollo. Assumes that the reader has at least a rough knowledge of the sequence of events; could serve as supplemental reading to Lewis's *Appointment on the Moon*. Includes a revealing interview with von Braun.

INDEX

921
VON BRAUN   Lampton,
            Christopher.

        Wernher von Braun

    $12.90   2438